vegetarian **indian**

vegetarian
indian

Shehzad Husain

Photography by Steve Baxter

hamlyn

ACKNOWLEDGEMENTS
Art Director **Jacqui Small**
Executive Art Editor **Penny Stock**
Designer **Louise Leffler**
Executive Editor **Susan Haynes**
Editors **Janice Anderson, Elsa Petersen-Schepelern, Kathy Steer**
Production Controller **Melanie Frantz**
Photographer **Steve Baxter**
Home Economist **Annie Nichols**
Stylist **Helen Payne**
Indexer **Hilary Bird**

First published in Great Britain in 1995
by Hamlyn
a division of Octopus Publishing Group Limited
2–4 Heron Quays, London, E14 4JP

This paperback edition first published 2001

NOTES
Both metric and imperial measurements have been given in all recipes.
Use one set of measurements only and not a mixture of both.
Standard level spoon measurements are used in all recipes.
1 tablespoon = one 15 ml spoon
1 teaspoon = one 5 ml spoon
Eggs should be size 3 unless otherwise stated.
Milk should be full fat unless otherwise stated.
Pepper should be freshly ground black pepper unless otherwise stated.
Fresh herbs should be used unless otherwise stated.
If unavailable use dried herbs as an alternative but halve the quantities stated.
Ovens should be preheated to the specified temperature – if using a fan-assisted oven,
follow the manufacturer's instructions for adjusting the time and the temperature.
Many Indian dishes are suitable for vegans, who should avoid recipes containing eggs,
cream or milk, yogurt or panir, and use vegetable ghee instead of butter or ghee.
Many recipes, other than those containing cracked wheat (page 35), wheat flour and other
wheat products, and chapati flour (made of wholemeal flour), are suitable for those on a
gluten-free diet. Gram flour or besun, in particular, is suitable since it is made from lentils.
Indian vegetarian meals can be adapted for any members of the family who are not
vegetarians, simply by adding another curry dish containing fish, poultry or meat.
Recipes serve 4, if served as part of a meal comprising several dishes.

ILLUSTRATION, *page 2: Indian breads, from the top, Besun Ki Roti*
(recipe page 103) and Chapati (recipe page 102).

Contents

Tamarind

Doodhi

Okra

Betel Leaf

Baby Aubergines

Red Chillies

Tinday

Coriander

Green Chilli

Karela (Bitter Gourd)

Green Mango

Doodhi

Fenugreek

Curry Leaves

Introduction

Vegetarian cooking in India is very highly developed, with a tradition going back thousands of years. It is largely based on religious principles. The major religious groups in the Indian sub-continent include Hindus, Muslims, Buddhists, Jains, Parsees, Sikhs, Jews and Christians. Many of these religions follow special dietary laws; Muslims and Jews do not eat pork, while Hindus never eat beef and rarely pork. Buddhists, some Hindu castes and Jains all have a long tradition of vegetarianism. Certain areas, such as Gujarat, Tamil Nadu and Kerala, are particularly well known for the quality of their vegetarian dishes.

Indian vegetarian cooking provides a wide variety of tastes. Its nutritional values are unsurpassed, and its variety is almost limitless, coming as it does from areas as diverse as the high Himalaya of Kashmir in the far north to the palm-fringed beaches of Kerala in the south, from the red deserts of Rajastan in the west to the jungles of Orissa in the east.

You will find in this book dishes from every corner of this huge and diverse country and recipes for the grandest and most sophisticated dinner party and for the most casual of takeaway snacks. In fact, India can be said to have virtually invented fast food – pakoras, samosas and chaat have been the 'eat-and-run' food of millions.

When serving an Indian meal, always provide more than one dish. Main vegetable curries should be accompanied by rice and/or bread, a dhaal (pulse) dish, one or more chutneys or pickles and perhaps a salad or raita. This will result in a meal which is nutritionally complete as well as delicious. You may find that some people like their dishes less spicy than others – for them, just decrease the quantity of chillies in the recipe.

The book is divided into courses, which is familiar to the Western style of eating. In India, however, all the dishes would be served at the same time. They are placed in the middle of the table, and the diners help themselves according to their taste and appetite.

In the north, breads such as naan and rotis are the staple foods, while in the south, rice is the basis of every meal. In addition, I have included a chapter on 'curries' although in India there is no such thing! 'Curry', however, is how people in the West think of 'main course' dishes in Indian cooking, so curry it is!

COOKING AND EATING VEGETARIAN FOOD

Store cupboard items

Your basic stock of spices should include fresh ginger and garlic, chilli powder, turmeric, cardamom, black pepper, ground coriander and cumin. The powdered spices will keep very well in airtight containers, carefully labelled, while the fresh ginger and garlic will keep for seven to ten days in the refrigerator. Other useful items, to be acquired as your repertoire increases, are cumin seeds (black and white), onion seeds, mustard seeds, cloves, cinnamon, dried red chillies, fenugreek, vegetable ghee and garam masala, a mixture of spices that can either be bought ready-made or made at home in quantity for use whenever required. The Ingredients section beginning on page 10 describes many of these items in greater detail.

Spices

It is a good idea, particularly if you are new to Indian cooking, to take out all the spices before you start cooking and keep them either on a plate or in small separate bowls. Chop onions and other vegetables before you start cooking.

Spices may be used whole or ground, roasted or fried, individually or mixed. One spice can completely alter the flavour of a dish and different combinations of several can produce a variety of colours and textures.

Many of the recipes in this book call for ground spices, which are generally available in supermarkets as well as in Indian and Pakistani grocers. In India, cooks almost always buy whole spices and grind them at home, and there is no doubt that freshly ground spices make a noticeable difference to the end product. However, it is quicker and more convenient to use ground spices.

For some of the recipes in this book, the spices must be roasted. In India, this would be done on a *thawa* (see page 122), but a heavy-based frying pan may be used instead. No water or oil is added to the spices; they are simply dry-roasted whole over a high heat while the pan is shaken to prevent them burning.

The quantities of spices given in the recipes in this book are merely a guide. Do not hesitate to increase the quantities if you wish, especially in the cases of salt and chilli powder, which are very much a matter of individual taste. Remember that long cooking over a lowish heat will always improve the taste of the food, as it allows the spices to be absorbed. This is why reheating a dish the following day is no problem with most Indian food, provided it has been kept in the refrigerator in the meantime. Do feel free to experiment with the different spices, especially chillies, since the hotness of a curry depends on the chilli content. Omit them, or decrease the quantity, if you find you can't tolerate a very hot curry.

Ginger and Garlic

Both ginger and garlic are frequently used in curries. Since it takes time and effort to peel and chop them, I suggest you take about 250 g (8 oz) of each, soak them separately overnight (this makes them easy to peel), peel and grind them separately in a food processor, adding a little water to form a pulp. The pulps can be stored separately in airtight containers in a cool place for a month or even longer, to be used as you need them.

Yogurt

Always use natural unsweetened yogurt. When adding this ingredient to curries, I always whip it first with a fork so that it does not curdle, then I add it gradually. Yogurt helps to tenderize the other ingredients and give curry a thick, creamy texture. Raita – yogurt sauce – also complements most curries beautifully.

The secret of a good curry

The final colour and texture of a curry will depend on how well you browned the onions in the first stage. This requires patience, especially if you are cooking a large quantity. Heat the oil first, add the onions, then reduce the heat slightly so that the onions become golden brown without burning, and stir them gently with a wooden spoon or spatula as they cook.

Once this is done, add the spices, vegetables or other ingredients of the curry you are making and mix and coat by *bhoono-ing* (stirring and frying in gently semicircular movements, scraping the bottom of the pan). This is essential for a good end-result. When you have done this you should taste the food and adjust the seasoning according to your own palate. Remember that the recipes are only guidelines, not prescriptions, so you do not have to follow them too rigidly.

Thickening sauces

In Indian cooking, flour is very rarely used to thicken sauces. Instead, Indian cooks rely on onions and spices (such as ginger, garlic or powdered coriander) to produce a thick brown sauce.

Making a baghaar (*seasoned oil dressing*)

As far as I know, this dressing is used only in Indian cooking. Oil or ghee is heated to a very high temperature without burning, and spices, onions and herbs are dropped into the oil, immediately changing colour and becoming very aromatic. The seasoned oil is then removed from the heat and poured over the dish – often a cooked dhaal or vegetables – like a dressing. Sometimes, raw food is also added to the heated oil, to be sautéed or simmered. You will find instructions for baghaar in the relevant recipes.

Freezing Indian food

The good thing about Indian food is that most of it freezes well, with very little loss of flavour. The potato is an exception, though, as it becomes mushy when cooked and frozen in a curry. If you are planning to cook and freeze a dish containing potato, leave out the potato and add it on the day you serve the dish.

To reheat on the day, defrost the dish thoroughly at room temperature for a few hours and then reheat as appropriate; the best ways to reheat a thawed curry are either in an oven, in a saucepan over a gentle heat on top of the stove, or under a grill, depending on the nature of the dish. Some dishes may be shallow-fried, but I find this makes the food a little too greasy. A microwave oven is, of course, the latest answer to thawing and reheating frozen dishes.

PRESENTATION

There are few rules about presenting Indian food, but if you are entertaining keep in mind which serving dishes you plan to use for each recipe, and do not neglect the final decorative touches – the fresh coriander leaves or the chopped chilli garnishes – that make the food look so appetizing. Curries and dhaal are best served in large, deep dishes, rice is piled on flat oval dishes and raita (yogurt sauce) is best served in a bowl or sauce boat. Breads such as chapatis, paratas or puris should be served on a plate wrapped in foil to keep them warm for as long as possible. Pickles, chutneys and kachumbers (fruits or vegetables with spices in lemon juice) are eaten in small portions, so it is best to put them in small bowls, each with a teaspoon in them, so that people do not take large helpings. In any case some of the pickles can be very hot and are certainly not intended to be eaten on their own or in large quantities.

Guests usually help themselves from the serving dishes. Rice is placed in the centre of the dinner plate, leaving some room for the curries, which are never put on top of the rice. It is not necessary to help yourself to everything on the table at once.

Though you may wish to provide a cruet set for the dinner table, it is a mistake for anyone to add salt before tasting, because the cook will always have added it with all the other spices during cooking. Garnishes, such as coriander leaves and green chillies, are best if fresh, though they may be prepared in advance and kept frozen in polythene bags or small freezer containers for convenience. Do not wash the coriander before freezing it; just rinse it under a cold tap before use. Coriander is easy to grow in the garden, especially during the summer months, and I have been reasonably successful growing it on the window sill; it is worthwhile growing your own coriander – it is not always easy to find. Other attractive and inexpensive garnishes include onion rings, tomatoes and lemon wedges.

By contrast, a special way of decorating savoury dishes or desserts is to use *varq* (beaten silver leaf, which is edible). This custom probably started with the Moghuls, seeking to intrigue their guests at palace banquets, and is reserved for special occasions because it is quite expensive. A dessert decorated with *varq* certainly looks beautiful, and is bound to impress your guests. It provides quite a talking point, but since it is real silver, it may not be very pleasant for people with fillings in their teeth.

Finally, if you want to clear your home of cooking smells after cooking Indian food, try lighting up a few incense sticks (*agarbathis*) about an hour before the guests are due. I find these are more effective than air fresheners, and they come in various fragrances, including jasmine and rose.

PLANNING MEALS

The dishes you choose will depend upon the occasion. For a supper party, for example, a biryani or khitchri would make a very good centrepiece, though for a family meal you might prefer something less elaborate. The important thing to bear in mind is that protein should always be included, perhaps panir, or a pulse; lentil dishes, usually served as dhaal, are good complements for most vegetarian curries. I have indicated in each recipe whether the curry is 'wet', that is with a sauce, or 'dry', and this should help you to combine textures for a varied spread.

Accompaniments such as chutneys and kachumbers are not a must, but I feel they perk up a meal; raitas are used to cool a hot curry or to freshen the palate. A typical vegetarian meal might consist of a vegetable curry, a lentil dish, a kachumber or chutney, rice and/or bhajias, followed by dessert. Usually, dishes are all served together, except for the dessert, following no particular order as in other cuisines – but of course this is up to you.

AN ABC OF INGREDIENTS

Asafoetida
A pale yellow spice with a strong, distinctive flavour, used in small quantities to enhance other flavours in a dish.

Aamchoor
Sour-tasting mango powder made from dried raw mangoes. It is sold in jars.

Ata
see Wholemeal flour.

Besun
see Gram flour.

Bhoonay chanay
Dried roasted chickpeas.

Bitter gourd (*karela*)
A bitter-tasting gourd with a very knobbly skin. They should be peeled and salted or blanched before cooking to reduce the bitter flavour.

Bundi
Small, round, pearl-sized drops made from green lentil flour, usually soaked in water before use.

Cardamom (*elaichi*)
This spice, native to India, is considered the second most expensive (after saffron). The pods can be used with or without their husks and have a slightly pungent but very aromatic taste. They come in three varieties: green, white and black. The green and white pods can be used in both sweet and savoury dishes or to flavour rice; the black pods are used only in savoury dishes.

Cassia
see Cinnamon.

Cayenne pepper
see Chilli powder.

Chana dhaal
Very similar in appearance to moong dhaal (yellow split peas) – this lentil has slightly less shiny grains. It is used as a binding agent.

Chana dhaal flour
see Gram flour.

Chapati flour
see Wholemeal flour.

Chilli powder (*laal mirch*) or cayenne pepper
Powdered dried red chillies. It is a very fiery spice that should be used with caution.

Chillies, dried red (*sabath sookhi laal mirch*)
These pods, available whole or crushed, are extremely fiery and should be used with caution; their effect can be toned down slightly by removing the seeds. Dried chillies are usually fried in oil before use.

Chillies, fresh green (*hari mirch*)
Very aromatic in flavour, these are used both in cooking, and as a garnish. Though now so closely identified with

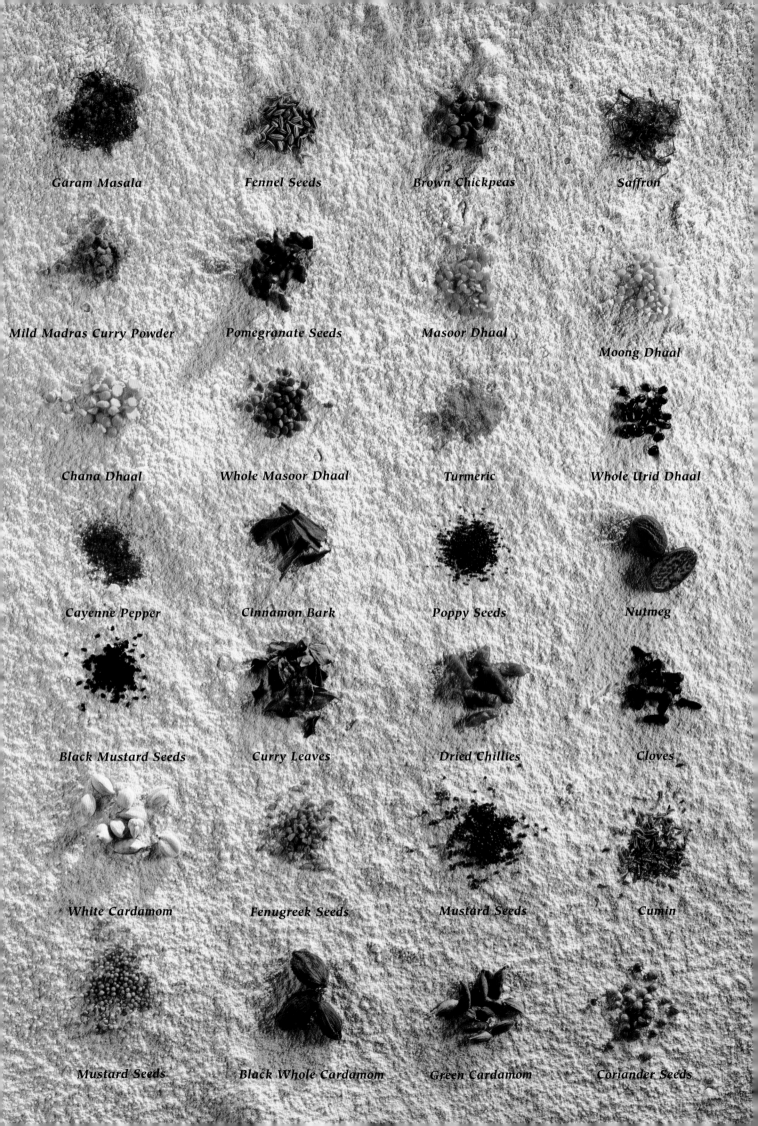

Garam Masala

Fennel Seeds

Brown Chickpeas

Saffron

Mild Madras Curry Powder

Pomegranate Seeds

Masoor Dhaal

Moong Dhaal

Chana Dhaal

Whole Masoor Dhaal

Turmeric

Whole Urid Dhaal

Cayenne Pepper

Cinnamon Bark

Poppy Seeds

Nutmeg

Black Mustard Seeds

Curry Leaves

Dried Chillies

Cloves

White Cardamom

Fenugreek Seeds

Mustard Seeds

Cumin

Mustard Seeds

Black Whole Cardamom

Green Cardamom

Coriander Seeds

Indian cooking, they were introduced to the country until the 16th Century, by the Portuguese. The seeds, which are the hottest part, may be removed if desired, by slitting the chilli down the middle. Never touch the face, especially the eyes or nose, during or after handling chillies; even after washing your hands it will sting.

Cinnamon (*dhalchini*)
One of the earliest-known spices, cinnamon comes from the bark of a tree grown mainly in Sri Lanka. It has an aromatic and sweet flavour. Sold both in powdered form and as sticks. The bark of the tree cinnamon comes from is sold as Cassia bark.

Cloves (*laung*)
Used to flavour many sweet and savoury dishes; usually added whole. A whole clove is sometimes used to seal a betel leaf for serving after an Indian meal (see Paan).

Coconut (*khopra or narial*)
Used to flavour sweet or savoury dishes, fresh coconut can often be bought in supermarkets. Desiccated coconut and creamed coconut are also available and for most dishes make acceptable substitutes. Coconut is sometimes toasted before cooking (as for spices, see page 8).

Coriander, fresh (*hara dhania*)
A fragrant herb used as an ingredient and as a garnish.

Coriander seeds (*dhania*)
This aromatic spice has a pungent, slightly lemony flavour. The seeds are used widely, either coarsely ground or powdered, in meat, fish and poultry dishes.

Corn oil
Less fattening than other oils, especially ghee, and also odourless, this is my preferred cooking oil.

Cumin, ground (*safaid zeera*)
A rather musty-smelling spice in its raw state, widely used for flavouring lentils and vegetable curries. Its flavour comes into its own when roasted or fried.

Cumin seeds (*shah zeera*)
Black cumin seeds, which have a strong aromatic flavour, are used to flavour curries and rice. White cumin seeds cannot be used as a substitute.

Curry leaves (*kari patta*)
Similar in appearance to bay leaves but very different in flavour. Available fresh (occasionally) or dried, they are used to flavour lentil dishes and vegetable curries.

Doodhi (*kaddu*)
A vegetable – a member of the squash family. It is shaped rather like a curved courgette and is generally pale green in colour. Marrow, squash or courgettes can be substituted.

Fennel seeds (*sonfe*)
Similar to white cumin, these have a sweet taste and are used to flavour certain curries. They can also be chewed (as betel nut and cardamom are) after a spicy meal.

Fenugreek (*methi*)
The flavour of the whole, dried, flat yellow seeds, a little bitter in taste, improves when they are lightly fried. Fresh fenugreek, sold in bunches, has very small leaves and is used to flavour both meat and vegetarian dishes.

Garam masala
A mixture of spices which can either be made up at home from freshly ground spices or bought ready made. There is no set formula, but a typical mixture might include black cumin seeds, peppercorns, cloves, cinnamon and black cardamom. To make your own mixture, grind together a 2.5 cm (1 inch) piece cinnamon stick, 3 cloves, 3 black peppercorns, 2 black cardamoms (with husks removed) and 2 teaspoons black cumin seeds. If desired, multiply the quantities, grind and store in an airtight jar for future use.

Garlic (*lassun*)
This very useful flavouring is frequently used in curries, especially with ginger. It can be puréed in large quantities in a food processor and kept in an airtight container in the refrigerator (see page 9). Whole garlic cloves are sometimes added to lentil dishes.

Ghee (*clarified butter*)
There are two kinds: pure (a dairy product) and vegetable. Though it was once a matter of pride to be able to claim that everything served in one's household was cooked in pure ghee, it is in fact quite high in cholesterol, so from the health standpoint it may be better to use vegetable ghee or vegetable oil wherever possible (the majority of curries are cooked in oil). To make pure ghee at home melt 250 g (8 oz) butter in a heavy saucepan and allow to simmer for 10–12 minutes. Once the milky white froth has turned golden, strain (preferably through muslin or cheesecloth) and store in a jar.

Ginger root (*adrak, fresh ginger, green ginger*)
One of the most popular flavourings in India and also one of the oldest, ginger is an important ingredient in many curries. It should always be peeled before use and can be puréed in a food processor (see page 9). Dried powdered ginger (*sontt*) is also useful to have in your larder.

Gram flour (*besun or chana dhaal flour*)
Made from lentils, gram flour is used to make pakoras, and can also be used as a binding agent. A combination of gram flour and ordinary wholemeal flour (*ata*, or chapati flour) makes a delicious Indian bread called *Besun Ki Roti* (see recipe, page 103). This kind of flour is also very useful for people who are allergic to gluten, a component of all wheat products.

Kaddu
see Doodhi.

Karela
see Bitter gourd.

Kewra water

This is the essence of pandanus or screwpine, used to flavour sweet dishes and sometimes rice. It is sold in small bottles. Its scent is rather reminiscent of vanilla, and a little vanilla essence may be substituted.

Mace

see Nutmeg.

Masoor dhaal

Small, round and pale orange in colour, these split lentils are stocked by all supermarkets, labelled simply 'lentils' or 'red lentils'.

Mooli

From the same family as the radish; long, rather like a cucumber, and white, mooli has a lovely flavour and a crunchy texture. It goes well with carrot.

Moong dhaal

This is a tear-drop-shaped yellow split lentil, more popular in northern India than in the south.

Mustard oil

Often used in Bengali dishes, especially for cooking fish.

Mustard seeds (*sarson ke beenji rai*)

These small round seeds, either black or yellow, are rather sharp in flavour. They are used in curries and pickles.

Nutmeg (*jaifal*)

Nutmeg, a native of Indonesia, is sweet and aromatic. Mace, with its slightly more subtle flavour, is the lacy covering on the nutmeg kernel.

Onion seeds (*kalongi*)

Black in colour and triangular in shape, these are used for both pickles and vegetable curries.

Paan

Betel leaf wrapped around calcium paste, cardamom and fennel seeds, etc., and held together with a clove and sometimes covered with *varq*. Served at the end of the meal as a mouth-freshener. It may contain tobacco, in which case it can be addictive. It can be bought or made at home.

Paprika

This powder, made from dried sweet red pepper, is known as a hot-flavoured spice, though it is much less fiery than chilli pepper. Paprika is not much used in Indian cookery.

Pepper

Whenever possible, use freshly ground black pepper in Indian cooking.

Pistachio nuts

Widely used in Indian desserts, these are not the salty type sold in their shells but the shelled ones sold in packets at all Indian and Pakistani grocers.

Poppy seeds (*khush khush*)

These dried whole seeds are always better when toasted. They are used, often whole, to flavour curries. Although they are from the opium poppy, they do not contain opium.

Rosewater

This is used mainly to flavour certain sweetmeats.

Saffron (*zafran*)

The world's most expensive spice has a uniquely beautiful flavour and fragrance. Made from the stigmas of the saffron crocus, native to Asia Minor, each 500 g (1 lb) of saffron needs 60,000 stigmas. Fortunately, only a small quantity is needed to flavour or colour a dish, whether sweet or savoury. Saffron is sold as strands or in powder form.

Sesame seeds (*thill*)

Whole, flat, cream-coloured seeds, these are used to flavour curries. When ground, sesame seeds can also be made into chutney.

Set

A spice mixture.

Sev

Very fine gram flour strands, used in *bhel poori*, which can be bought in Indian and Pakistani grocers.

Sontt

see Ginger root.

Tamarind (*imli*)

The dried pods of the tamarind, or Indian date. They are sour tasting and very sticky. Tamarind has to be soaked in hot water to extract the flavour. Though it is much stronger than lemon, lemon is often used as a substitute. Nowadays tamarind can be bought in paste form in jars: mix with a little water to bring it to a runny consistency.

Toor dhaal

Split pigeon peas; larger and more yellow than moong dhaal (see above).

Turmeric (*haled*)

This bright yellow, bitter-tasting spice is sold ground. It is used mainly for colour, rather than flavour.

Urid dhaal

Though very similar in shape and size to moong dhaal, this lentil is white and a little drier when cooked. It is popular in northern India.

Urid dhaal flour

This very fine white flour is used for vadde (deep-fried dumplings – recipe on page 111), and for dosas (Indian rice pancakes).

Varq

Edible silver leaf used for decoration purposes. It is very delicate and should be handled carefully. It can be bought in sheets from Indian or Pakistani grocers, though you may have to order it in advance.

Wholemeal flour (*ata*)

Chapati flour, available at any Indian or Pakistani grocer's shop, is used to make chapatis, paratas and puris. Ordinary wholemeal flour may also be used for Indian breads, very well sieved.

Starters and Snacks

The dishes in this chapter may be served
Indian-style – that is, at the same time as the curry
and lentil dishes in a meal – or Western-style, as
something to whet the appetite while the main
courses are being completed. Either way, they are
delicious. Many of them also make perfect snacks,
or form the basis for light, middle-of-the-day meals.

Baby Potatoes in Mint

These can be served as a starter with a crisp salad (see pages 111–113) – but they are also perfect as an accompaniment for other curry and pulse dishes. The flavours also go very well with European vegetarian dishes. Choose any small potato variety, such as Jersey Royals, the yellow, waxy, French varieties such as Ratte, or the delightfully named Pink Fir Apples.

20–25 BABY POTATOES
125 G (4 OZ) UNSALTED BUTTER
½ TEASPOON GARLIC PULP
3 GREEN CHILLIES, FINELY CHOPPED
3 TABLESPOONS CHOPPED FRESH MINT
3 TABLESPOONS CHOPPED FRESH CORIANDER
1½ TEASPOONS SALT
3 TABLESPOONS LEMON JUICE

Wash and slice the potatoes thickly, then boil them in lightly salted water until they are soft but not mushy, so they retain their shape.

Melt the butter in a small saucepan and add the garlic, green chillies, mint, coriander, salt and lemon juice. Blend together in the pan before pouring the mixture over the potatoes.

Serve immediately.

Baked Baby Potato Chaat

This makes a delicious starter. You should serve about three or four per person. In India, there are shops devoted to selling various kinds of chaats. You mix the chaat spices to your own individual taste and sprinkle them over the food. Chaat spices include salt, chilli powder, ginger and ground, roasted cumin seeds. Chaats are delicious when eaten with glasses of lassi (see pages 26 and 120). Although lemon juice may be used instead of tamarind, the latter is such an intrinsic part of this dish it is better not to replace it.

16 BABY POTATOES
175 ML (6 FL OZ) BOILING WATER
250 G (8 OZ) RED TAMARIND BLOCK
3 TABLESPOONS TOMATO SAUCE
1 TEASPOON CHILLI POWDER
1 TEASPOON SALT
1 TEASPOON GINGER POWDER
2 TABLESPOONS SUGAR
1 TABLESPOON CHOPPED FRESH MINT
1 TABLESPOON CHOPPED FRESH CORIANDER
2 TABLESPOONS NATURAL YOGURT, WHISKED
2 TABLESPOONS WATER
TO GARNISH
1 SMALL ONION, DICED
1 TABLESPOON CHOPPED FRESH CORIANDER
2 GREEN CHILLIES, CHOPPED
1 TOMATO, DICED

Wash and prick the potatoes and bake in a hot oven, 200°C (400°F), Gas Mark 6, until cooked.

Meanwhile, pour the boiling water over the tamarind block. Once the water is cool, squeeze the pulp out of the tamarind and push it through a sieve. Blend this with the tomato sauce, and then mix in the chilli powder, salt, ginger powder, sugar, mint and coriander.

Pour the tamarind sauce over the potatoes and garnish with the diced onion, coriander, chopped chillies and diced tomato.

For the yogurt sauce, mix the yogurt and the water together in a small bowl, adding a little salt to taste. Serve the chaat cold with the yogurt sauce poured over the top.

PREVIOUS PAGES: From left, Mixed Chaat with Tamarind Chutney (recipe page 26) and Fried Moong Dhaal (recipe page 22). There are special chaat shops in India – you choose your dish, then sprinkle it with the chaat spices. Lassi, often tamarind-flavoured, is traditionally drunk with the chaat, so tamarind chutney is an appropriate accompaniment. Slightly salted Fried Moong Dhaal is good to nibble with drinks.

RIGHT: The potato is native to Peru, and was only discovered in 1534 by Pizarro, who brought it to Europe. It has been enthusiastically adopted by cooks all over the Indian sub-continent and has become a staple food in some areas, such as the high Himalaya. Illustrated from the top are Baby Potatoes in Mint (recipe above), Bombay Aloo (recipe on page 18), and Baked Baby Potato Chaat (recipe above, right).

Bombay Aloo

Illustrated on the previous page, Bombay Aloo is one of the most popular potato dishes in the Indian culinary repertoire, especially in the West. It can be eaten as a snack or served as a starter with one of the salads from this book on pages 111–113. This recipe is good made with any small potato variety, but I like it very much with the little, waxy, yellow ones, sometimes sold simply as 'Mediterranean potatoes', or salad potatoes. These will hold their shape better than the floury kind.

12–14 BABY POTATOES
2 TABLESPOONS TOMATO PURÉE
1 TEASPOON GROUND CORIANDER
1 TEASPOON CHILLI POWDER
1 TEASPOON SALT
1 TEASPOON SUGAR
2 TABLESPOONS LEMON JUICE
1 TABLESPOON OIL
½ TEASPOON MUSTARD SEEDS
6 CURRY LEAVES
1 TABLESPOON CHOPPED FRESH CORIANDER, TO GARNISH

Boil the baby potatoes with their skins on and cut them in half once cooked. Place in a serving dish.

Meanwhile, in a small bowl mix together the tomato purée, ground coriander, chilli powder, salt, sugar, and lemon juice.

Heat the oil in a small frying pan over a medium heat and gently fry the mustard seeds and curry leaves. Reduce the heat and add the tomato purée and spice mixture to the pan. Fry for about 1 minute then pour the hot mixture over the potatoes. Mix in carefully. Before serving, garnish the dish with chopped fresh coriander.

VARIATION
Bombay Aloo with Panir
Panir (see recipe on page 74) is a delicious addition to this dish. Just before serving, slice the panir, fry it lightly in ghee or butter, then add to the other ingredients.

To serve, finely slice 2 green chillies and scatter over, then garnish with sprigs of mint.

Masala Potato Wedges

A great snack at any time of the day, and also excellent as a starter with a crisp green salad, or as a nibble with drinks (serve it with the yogurt dip described below). This dish can be teamed with the Spicy Mushroom and Coriander Omelette on page 24 as a light lunch.

3 POTATOES, CUT LENGTHWAYS INTO QUARTERS
2 TABLESPOONS WATER
2 TABLESPOONS TOMATO PURÉE
3 TABLESPOONS LEMON JUICE
1 TEASPOON SALT
1 TEASPOON CHILLI POWDER
1½ TEASPOONS GROUND CORIANDER
1 TEASPOON GROUND CUMIN
2 TABLESPOONS CORN OIL
1 TABLESPOON CHOPPED FRESH CORIANDER, TO GARNISH

Boil the potatoes in lightly salted water until they are cooked, but still firm. Do not boil them until soft as they will be cooked further when coated in spices and roasted.

In a bowl, mix the water, tomato purée, lemon juice, salt and all the spices together to make a smooth paste. Brush a large, ovenproof dish with oil, add the potato wedges and pour over the spice mixture, coating them thoroughly but not too heavily.

Bake in a preheated moderate oven, 180°C (350°F), Gas Mark 4, for 20–25 minutes. Serve hot, sprinkled with the chopped fresh coriander, to garnish.

VARIATIONS
Masala Aubergines, Courgettes or Carrots
Cut small aubergines into wedges, or large ones into slices. Cut courgettes into thick batons or carrots into smaller ones. Parboil the vegetables and proceed as in the main recipe.

Yogurt Sauce for Masala Potatoes, Aubergines, Courgettes or Carrots
Delicious with drinks – a selection of Masala Wedges of Potatoes, Aubergines, Courgettes or Carrots served with a yogurt sauce. Mix 125 g (4 oz) Greek or home-made yogurt with ½ teaspoon salt, 1 teaspoon sugar, 1 tablespoon chopped fresh coriander leaves and 1–2 chopped fresh green chillies. Use 1 chilli for a milder sauce and 2 if your guests like it spicy.

Vegetable Cutlets

Cutlets were first introduced into Indian cooking by Indian cooks working for British Raj households, in an attempt to approximate dishes familiar to Europeans. They are also made with meat, but this now-traditional vegetarian version is truly wonderful.

2 LARGE POTATOES

125 G (4 OZ) PEAS

2 LARGE CARROTS, FINELY DICED

50 G (2 OZ) SWEETCORN KERNELS

1 ONION, CHOPPED

1½ TEASPOONS GARAM MASALA

1 TEASPOON CHILLI POWDER

2 RED CHILLIES, CHOPPED

2 TABLESPOONS CHOPPED FRESH CORIANDER

1½ TEASPOONS SALT

1 EGG, BEATEN (OPTIONAL)

175–250 G (6–8 OZ) BREADCRUMBS

OIL FOR SHALLOW-FRYING

Cook the potatoes in boiling salted water until they are well cooked but not mushy. Mash and set aside.

Boil the peas, carrots, sweetcorn and onion together in lightly salted water. When they are all cooked, drain thoroughly and gently mash them down.

Mix all the vegetables with the garam masala, chilli powder, red chillies, fresh coriander and salt.

Taste, and adjust the seasoning, before breaking off small balls of the mixture, about the size of a golf ball, to form small cutlets in the palms of your hands.

Place the beaten egg, if using, in a shallow dish and the breadcrumbs in another. Roll the cutlets first in the beaten egg (optional), then in the breadcrumbs, coating them thoroughly.

Heat the oil in a frying pan and shallow-fry the cutlets for about 1 minute, turning once.

Serve as a starter, accompaniment or snack.

Potato and Onion Cutlets
(Aloo Aur Pyaaz Kay Cutlets)

'Aloo' is the Hindi and Urdu word for potato – worthwhile remembering if you're trying to find your way around the menu in an Indian restaurant. These little 'potato balls' can be served as a starter, or even as an appetizer with drinks. To make the ginger pulp, either grate it finely, or purée the fresh root in the spice grinder, or sprinkle it with a little salt and mash it to a pulp with the point of a heavy knife.

4 LARGE POTATOES, PEELED AND DICED

1 TEASPOON GINGER PULP

2 TEASPOONS MANGO POWDER

2 TEASPOONS CHILLI POWDER

3 GREEN CHILLIES, CHOPPED

3 TABLESPOONS FRESH MINT, CHOPPED

4 TABLESPOONS FRESH CORIANDER, CHOPPED

2 TEASPOONS SALT

600 ML (1 PINT) CORN OIL

2 ONIONS, DICED

¼ TEASPOON ONION SEEDS

2 EGGS, LIGHTLY BEATEN

250–300 G (8–10 OZ) BREADCRUMBS

Boil the potato dice in lightly salted water and, when cooked, mash them, leaving some lumpy pieces.

Blend together the ginger pulp, mango powder, chilli powder, chopped green chillies, mint, coriander and salt in either a spice grinder or a food processor. Add this mixture to the mashed potato and set aside.

Heat 2 tablespoons of the oil in a frying pan and fry the onions with the onion seeds until golden brown. Remove the pan from the heat and allow to cool. Using a slotted spoon, remove the onions and pour on to the potato mixture, and with your hands, mix together thoroughly.

Break off small balls from the potato and onion mixture. Pat them between the palms of your hand, to form flat, round shapes about 2.5 cm (1 inch) thick. You should get about 10–12 cutlets.

Dip the potato cutlets in the beaten eggs then roll them in the breadcrumbs, coating them thoroughly. Heat the remaining oil in a frying pan and shallow-fry the cutlets over a medium heat in 2 or 3 batches until golden brown, turning them at least once during cooking.

Serve hot either as a starter or as an accompaniment.

Buttered Vegetables

These vegetables make an excellent accompaniment to almost anything – even a fried egg.

2 COURGETTES, SLICED (ABOUT 5 MM/¼ INCH THICK)
2 CARROTS, SLICED
½ CAULIFLOWER, BROKEN INTO FLORETS
1 GREEN PEPPER, DESEEDED AND SLICED
125 G (4 OZ) BUTTER
1 TEASPOON SALT
1 TABLESPOON CHOPPED FRESH CORIANDER
1 TEASPOON GARLIC PULP
1 TEASPOON CRUSHED DRIED RED CHILLIES

Place the vegetables in a large serving dish. Put the butter with the salt, coriander, garlic and crushed red chillies in a small saucepan. Melt over a high heat then pour over the vegetables. Toss and serve immediately.

Creamy Buttered Saag Panir

A sumptuous variation of the recipe above, which can also be served as part of the main course.

1 KG (2 LB) FRESH SPINACH, WASHED AND CHOPPED FINELY
12–14 CUBES PANIR, 2.5 CM (1 INCH) SQUARE
125 G (4 OZ) BUTTER
¼ TEASPOON ONION SEEDS
4 CURRY LEAVES
½ TEASPOON GARLIC PULP
½ TEASPOON POWDERED GINGER
1 TEASPOON CHILLI POWDER
½ TEASPOON SALT
150 ML (¼ PINT) SINGLE CREAM
1 TABLESPOON LEMON JUICE
2 FRESH RED CHILLIES, CHOPPED

Place the spinach in a saucepan with just the water clinging to the leaves and steam until wilted.

Heat 25 g (1 oz) of the butter in a small frying pan and fry the cubes of panir until lightly browned on all sides. Place the spinach and panir in a small serving dish and mix carefully.

Melt the remaining butter in a small pan, add the remaining ingredients except the lemon juice and chillies, then pour over the spinach and panir. Sprinkle with lemon juice, scatter over the chopped red chillies, then serve.

Mushroom and Leek Bhajias

'First cousins' to pakoras, bhajias can be made from many different kinds of vegetables. These make an ideal snack any time of the day. Serve them with the Spicy Tomato Ketchup on page 117.

250 G (8 OZ) GRAM FLOUR
1 TEASPOON SALT
½ TEASPOON BICARBONATE OF SODA
1 TEASPOON POMEGRANATE SEEDS
1 TEASPOON WHITE CUMIN SEEDS
1½ TEASPOONS CRUSHED RED CHILLIES
¼ TEASPOON TURMERIC
3 GREEN CHILLIES
250 G (8 OZ) MUSHROOMS, SLICED
2 LEEKS, CLEANED AND SLICED
1 TEASPOON CRUSHED CORIANDER SEEDS
2 TABLESPOONS CHOPPED FRESH CORIANDER
WATER TO MIX
SUFFICIENT OIL FOR DEEP-FRYING

Sieve the gram flour, salt and bicarbonate of soda into a medium bowl. Add the pomegranate seeds, white cumin seeds and crushed red chillies. Mix together and then add the turmeric, green chillies, mushrooms, leeks, coriander seeds, and the fresh coriander.

Add sufficient water to make a batter, about the consistency of a pancake mixture (like double cream). Set aside for about 10 minutes.

Meanwhile, heat the oil either in a karahi or a deep frying pan to 180°C (350°F), or until a cube of bread browns in 30 seconds. Using a tablespoon, drop spoonfuls of the batter mixture into the hot oil and fry quickly. When each bhajia looks quite firm at the bottom, turn over with a slotted spoon.

Reduce the heat to medium if the oil becomes too hot.

Once the bhajias are cooked right through, remove them and drain on absorbent kitchen paper to absorb any excess oil.

Serve the bhajias hot, ideally as they are being fried, with a spicy ketchup.

VARIATION
Onion Bhajias
One of the best-known Indian starters or snacks. Substitute 250–300 g (8–10 oz) of sliced onions for the mushrooms and leeks, and proceed as in the main recipe.

LEFT: *Above, Buttered Vegetables (recipe above, left) and Mushroom and Leek Bhajias (recipe above). Bhajias can be made from many different vegetables, including onions (see variation, above) and courgettes, cauliflower, peppers and chillies (see recipe on page 44).*

Dosai

A southern dish now popular all over India. Serve with a chutney or a spicy vegetable filling (masala dosa). Dosa flour, now widely available in Indian grocers, can be substituted for the rice and dhaal.

250 G (8 OZ) RICE OR GROUND RICE
50 G (2 OZ) URID DHAAL OR URID DHAAL FLOUR
1 TEASPOON SALT
4 TABLESPOONS CORN OR VEGETABLE OIL

Pick over the urid dhaal and discard any stones or twigs. Soak the rice and dhaal for at least 3 hours, then grind smoothly. Add water to give a batter-like consistency. If using ground rice and urid dhaal flour – or dosa flour – just mix with water to a similar consistency. Set aside for a further 3 hours to ferment.

Heat 1 tablespoon oil in a large, preferably non-stick pan. Pour in the rice mixture, and tilt to spread the batter over the base. Cover and cook for 2 minutes. Remove the lid, turn over the dosa and cook for a further 2 minutes, pouring a little oil around the edge. Serve with a chutney.

Fried Moong Dhaal

Moong dhaal is made from dried mung beans – those same mung beans which produce the bean sprouts used in Chinese and other oriental cuisines. Both varieties, the brown and the yellow, are enormously popular in Indian cooking. The yellow one has been husked and split, the brown just split. In this recipe, the moong dhaal is fried until crisp. It is just salted so has a subtle taste and is ideal for serving with drinks.

250 G (8 OZ) YELLOW MOONG DHAAL
1.2 LITRES (2 PINTS) WATER
300 ML (½ PINT) CORN OIL
1 TEASPOON SALT

Wash the moong dhaal thoroughly and soak it in the water for several hours, ideally overnight.

Drain off the liquid and leave the moong dhaal aside in a strainer so all the liquid is drained off.

When thoroughly drained, heat the oil in a karahi or a deep frying pan and start frying the dhaal in small quantities.

Using a slotted spoon, lift the fried moong dhaal out of the pan and drain it on absorbent kitchen paper.

When all the dhaal is fried, sprinkle salt on top and serve. When cool, the dhaal may be stored in plastic bags in the store cupboard for 2–3 weeks.

Illustrated on page 15.

Bombay Mix
(Chewra)

Bombay Mix consists of split peas with flaked rice, cashews and raisins. Mixes like this are served at any time of day, with drinks or tea. You can make a large quantity and store in an airtight container as a change from crisps. If you have any difficulty obtaining curry leaves, just omit them.

50 G (2 OZ) PEAS
300 ML (½ PINT) CORN OIL
½ TEASPOON ONION SEEDS
½ TEASPOON FENNEL SEEDS
6 CURRY LEAVES
250 G (8 OZ) FLAKED RICE (PAWA)
25 G (1 OZ) CASHEW NUTS
25 G (1 OZ) RAISINS
75 G (3 OZ) SUGAR
1 TEASPOON SALT
1 TEASPOON CHILLI POWDER

Heat the oil in a saucepan and fry the onion seeds, fennel seeds and curry leaves. Add the peas. Add the flaked rice and fry until crisp and golden (making sure the mixture doesn't burn). Using a slotted spoon, remove the mixture from the pan and place on a small tray lined with kitchen paper to absorb any excess oil. Tip the mixture into a bowl. Fry the cashew nuts in the remaining oil, remove with a slotted spoon and mix with the flaked rice. Then add the raisins, sugar, salt and chilli powder and mix well. Serve Bombay Mix immediately, or store in an airtight container.

Deep-fried Okra

Okra is known as 'bhindi' in India, and 'ladies' fingers' in parts of the Middle East. It is a favourite ingredient in Indian vegetarian cooking. Okra is a well-travelled vegetable – you find it also in Africa, and in American Creole cookery. Fried as in this recipe, okra makes a delicious, crispy accompaniment to any meal, and an interesting snack on its own, or with drinks. When choosing okra, make sure the pods are as fresh and young as possible. Check the stalk end, which should be green and firm. The pods themselves should also be quite firm. Bend them a little, and reject them if they show any signs of flabbiness.

500 G (1 LB) OKRA

300 ML (½ PINT) OIL

½ TEASPOON SALT

TO GARNISH

2–3 SPRIGS FRESH CORIANDER

4 LEMON WEDGES

Wash the whole okra and dry thoroughly on absorbent kitchen paper. Trim and cut them into 1 cm (½ inch) thick pieces.

Heat the oil in a karahi or deep frying pan and fry the okra in batches until crisp. Remove with a slotted spoon and drain on absorbent kitchen paper.

Once all the okra is fried, transfer to a serving dish, sprinkle with salt and serve garnished with the coriander sprigs and lemon wedges.

VARIATION

Deep-fried Cauliflower and Potato

For the okra, substitute 250 g (8 oz) potatoes, peeled and diced into 1 cm (½ inch) cubes and about 250 g (8 oz) cauliflower, broken into small florets. Fry the vegetables as in the main recipe, transfer to a serving dish, then sprinkle with 1 teaspoon white cumin seeds and garnish with fresh coriander.

Spicy Vegetable Selection

This is a delicious mix of different vegetables – you can vary it according to which vegetables look freshest and juiciest at your greengrocers. However, I do think that the peppers are crucial to the mix, so don't omit them on any account – and they are available in wonderful colours these days, including yellow and purple. Don't feel that this recipe can only be used as a starter, however – it is also perfect served as an accompaniment to other curries, and with Thali, the traditional South Indian dish on page 75.

2 COURGETTES

1 AUBERGINE

2 LARGE POTATOES

2 CARROTS

1 GREEN PEPPER, HALVED AND DESEEDED

1 RED PEPPER, HALVED AND DESEEDED

1 ORANGE PEPPER, HALVED AND DESEEDED

3 GREEN CHILLIES, FINELY CHOPPED

2 TABLESPOONS CHOPPED FRESH CORIANDER

1 TEASPOON GROUND CORIANDER

2 TEASPOONS MANGO POWDER

2 TABLESPOONS LEMON JUICE

1½ TEASPOONS SALT

2 TABLESPOONS OLIVE OIL

Cut all the vegetables into thick pieces: courgettes 2.5 cm (1 inch) thick slices; aubergine 2.5 cm (1 inch) thick slices; potatoes cut into wedges lengthways; carrots 2.5 cm (1 inch) thick pieces; peppers diced into large pieces.

Once all the vegetables are prepared, blanch the potatoes and carrots so they are cooked but not too soft and then transfer to a flameproof dish.

Mix the green chillies, fresh coriander, ground coriander, mango powder, lemon juice, salt and olive oil together in a small bowl. Pour over the vegetables and with a brush, spread the mixture over, coating the vegetables thoroughly.

Heat the grill to the hottest temperature, lower it to medium and grill the vegetables, basting occasionally with the oil and spice mixture, for 7–10 minutes. Serve hot.

Spicy Mushroom and Coriander Omelette

In India, omelettes usually just have onion, chillies and coriander as flavourings and are eaten mostly at breakfast or brunches. Do try this recipe with mushrooms as it is delicious, especially when served with Masala Potato Wedges (recipe page 18).

2 TOMATOES

1 SMALL ONION, FINELY CHOPPED

1 X 2.5 CM (1 INCH) PIECE FRESH GINGER, SHREDDED

1 LEVEL TEASPOON CRUSHED DRIED RED CHILLIES

1 TABLESPOON CHOPPED FRESH CORIANDER

1 TEASPOON SALT

2 GREEN CHILLIES, ROUGHLY CHOPPED

4 MUSHROOMS, SLICED

4 EGGS, LIGHTLY BEATEN

2 TABLESPOONS CORN OIL

Cut the tops off the tomatoes and remove as much pulp as possible. Dice roughly and place in a large mixing bowl.

Using a fork, thoroughly mix the onion, ginger, crushed red chillies, coriander, salt and green chillies and then add to the diced tomatoes.

Add the sliced mushrooms, then the beaten eggs and whisk everything together.

Heat half the oil in a large frying pan and add half of the egg mixture. Fry until cooked, turning once. Remove the omelette from the pan and keep warm on a serving plate. Heat the remaining oil in the pan, add the remaining egg mixture and make a second omelette.

Serve the omelettes with Masala Potato Wedges, if liked.

VARIATION

Omelette with Fresh Red Chillies or Peppers

For a very colourful version of this recipe, substitute 2 roughly chopped red chillies for the green. If you prefer your omelette a little less spicy, substitute finely diced red pepper.

Thick Spicy Vegetable Soup

Soup was not very common in Indian cuisine. However, Indian cooks are now developing their own soup recipes, and this one is a delicious example. It is almost like a broth and is very warming on a cold winter's day.

1 SMALL ONION

1 CARROT

2 MUSHROOMS

1 POTATO

125 G (4 OZ) PEAS

1 TEASPOON TOMATO PURÉE

300 ML (½ PINT) WATER

1 TABLESPOON CORN OIL

1 LARGE PINCH ONION SEEDS

½ TEASPOON GROUND CORIANDER

½ TEASPOON GARAM MASALA

½ TEASPOON CHILLI POWDER

1 TEASPOON CHOPPED FRESH CORIANDER

1 TABLESPOON CORNFLOUR

2 TEASPOONS LEMON JUICE

4 TABLESPOONS SINGLE CREAM

1 TEASPOON SALT

FRESH CORIANDER SPRIGS, TO GARNISH

Peel and dice the onion, carrot, mushrooms and potato very finely and place in a large bowl.

Add the peas to the vegetables, mix in the tomato purée and pour in 150 ml (¼ pint) of the water to loosen the mixture.

Heat the oil in a karahi or deep frying pan and fry the onion seeds until they turn a shade darker. Lower the heat, add the vegetable mixture and stir into the oil. Add the ground coriander, garam masala, chilli powder and fresh coriander.

Mix the cornflour with the remaining water and pour on to the vegetables in the pan. Stir and cook for about 2 minutes, then pour in the lemon juice and mix thoroughly. Finally, stir in the cream and add salt to taste.

Transfer to a warmed serving dish and serve garnished with coriander sprigs.

RIGHT: *From top, Thick Spicy Vegetable Soup (recipe above, right) is deliciously warming on a cold winter's day, while Spicy Mushroom and Coriander Omelette (recipe above), is an unusual variation on the more common breakfast omelette and includes onion, chillies and coriander. Substitute red pepper for the chillies if you prefer a milder taste.*

Mixed Chaat with Tamarind Chutney

Chaat shops are very popular in India. Customers sprinkle the chaat spices over their chosen dishes, while the delicious, cooling yogurt drink, lassi, flavoured with tamarind, is the usual accompaniment. Here, that same fresh-tasting tamarind is used to make the chutney which accompanies the chaat.

300 ML (½ PINT) NATURAL YOGURT

125 ML (4 FL OZ) WATER

2 TABLESPOONS SUGAR

1½ TEASPOONS SALT

2 POTATOES, PEELED AND ROUGHLY DICED

1 X 425 G (14 OZ) CAN CHICKPEAS

PASTRY SQUARES

175 G (6 OZ) SELF-RAISING FLOUR

1 TEASPOON SALT

¼ TEASPOON WHITE CUMIN SEEDS

50 G (2 OZ) BUTTER

WATER (SEE METHOD)

CORN OIL, FOR DEEP-FRYING

TAMARIND CHUTNEY

175 G (6 OZ) RED TAMARIND BLOCK

300 ML (½ PINT) WATER

½ TEASPOON POWDERED GINGER

2 TABLESPOONS SUGAR

1 TEASPOON CHILLI POWDER

1 TEASPOON SALT

2 TABLESPOONS TOMATO SAUCE

TO GARNISH

1 TABLESPOON CHOPPED FRESH CORIANDER

1 TABLESPOON PEANUTS

1 TABLESPOON SET (OPTIONAL)

Place the yogurt, water, sugar and salt together in a large bowl whisk well and set aside. Boil the potato dice until soft, drain well and set aside. Drain the can of chickpeas and add to the cooked potatoes.

To make the pastry squares, sift the flour and salt into a large mixing bowl. Mix in the cumin seeds and rub in the butter, using your fingertips. Add sufficient water to form a soft dough. Let the dough stand for about 10 minutes before rolling it out on a lightly floured surface to about 3 mm (⅛ inch) thick. Using a pastry cutter, cut the pastry into 2.5 cm (1 inch) squares. (You should get about 10–12 squares.) Set aside on a floured surface. To deep-fry the squares, heat sufficient oil in a frying pan or karahi over a moderate heat. Fry the squares in batches, turning them at least twice. When they are a golden brown, remove from the pan with a slotted spoon and drain on absorbent kitchen paper.

To make the tamarind chutney, boil the tamarind in water for 7–10 minutes. Place the tamarind block in a sieve and press down with a spoon to form a thick pulp. Add a little water to make a thick sauce, then add the ginger, sugar, chilli powder, salt and tomato sauce. When the mixture is thoroughly blended, set the sauce aside.

To serve the mixed chaat, divide the potato and chickpea mixture between 4 individual plates. Spread the pastry squares on top. Spoon the yogurt sauce and tamarind chutney over the pastry. Garnish each plate with fresh coriander, peanuts and a sprinkle of set, if liked. Serve the mixed chaat cold, with the Rosewater-flavoured Lassi (recipe below).

Illustrated on page 14.

Rosewater-flavoured Lassi, with Chopped Pistachio Nuts

Lassi is traditionally served in chaat shops in India. There are many different lassi recipes, some sweet and some salty. This one, flavoured with saffron or rosewater and sprinkled with chopped, unsalted, raw pistachios, is absolutely sumptuous!

300 ML (½ PINT) NATURAL YOGURT

600 ML (1 PINT) WATER

1 TEASPOON ROSEWATER, OR TO TASTE

2 TEASPOONS CHOPPED, FRESH PISTACHIO NUTS

(OPTIONAL)

Place the yogurt in a jug and whisk with a wire whisk for about 2 minutes. Pour in the water, sugar and rosewater. Continue to whisk for a further 3–5 minutes.

Serve chilled, sprinkled with chopped pistachios, if liked.

VARIATION

Saffron-flavoured Lassi

Instead of the rosewater, substitute 1 pinch of saffron threads, steeped for about 30 minutes in a little water, and continue as in the main recipe.

Serve with or without the pistachio nuts.

Curry Puffs with Vegetable Pastry

Curry Puffs can be served hot as a starter or at a drinks party. They are also suitable for a light lunch when served with a salad – and, when cold, absolutely ideal for taking on picnics, or as a packed lunch.

1 POTATO, DICED
½ CAULIFLOWER, CUT INTO FLORETS
50 G (2 OZ) FROZEN PEAS
50 G (2 OZ) GREEN BEANS, SLICED
2 TABLESPOONS TOMATO PURÉE
1 TABLESPOON LEMON JUICE
1 TEASPOON GARLIC PULP
1 TEASPOON GINGER PULP
1½ TEASPOONS CHILLI POWDER
1 TEASPOON GROUND CORIANDER
1 TEASPOON GARAM MASALA
1 TEASPOON SALT
4 TABLESPOONS CORN OIL
½ TEASPOON WHITE CUMIN SEEDS
1 ONION, DICED
150 ML (¼ PINT) WATER
6 TABLESPOONS DOUBLE CREAM
1 TABLESPOON CHOPPED FRESH CORIANDER
1 EGG, WHISKED
ROUGH PUFF PASTRY
275 G (9 OZ) PLAIN FLOUR
½ TEASPOON SALT
175 G (6 OZ) BUTTER
150 ML (5 FL OZ) WATER

Put all the prepared vegetables in a bowl, cover with water and set aside.

Meanwhile, mix the tomato purée, lemon juice, garlic, ginger, chilli powder, ground coriander, garam masala and salt in a small bowl.

Heat the oil in a heavy-based saucepan and fry the white cumin seeds and onion until golden brown. Lower the heat, stir in the tomato purée mixture and stir-fry for about 3 minutes.

Drain the potato, cauliflower, peas and beans and add to the saucepan. Stir well. Pour in the measured water, cover and cook for about 3–5 minutes, until the vegetables are cooked. Remove the lid and continue cooking, stirring, until the liquid has been fully absorbed, then pour in the cream and add the fresh coriander.

Cook for a further 3–5 minutes, so that the sauce has thickened. Set the sauce aside to cool while you make the rough puff pastry.

For the pastry, sift the flour and salt into a large mixing bowl. Cut the butter into small cubes and drop these on to the flour,

covering them fully with the flour. Begin to stir the measured water in gradually, mixing to form a soft dough.

Set the dough aside in a cool place for about 15 minutes.

Roll out the pastry on a lightly floured board. Fold the pastry into half, roll out again and repeat this process again so you end up with 2–3 layers.

Start to break off small balls (about 4-6 depending on the size of the curry puffs you want) and roll these out into a rounds about 10–12 cm (4–5 inches) across. Put tablespoonfuls of the vegetable curry mixture on one half of each round. Dampen the edges with water slightly and fold over into pasty shapes. Brush with the whisked egg. When all the pastries are ready, place on an ovenproof dish and bake in a preheated moderate oven, 180°C (350°F), Gas Mark 4, for about 15–20 minutes.

Spicy Mushroom and Fresh Coriander Soup

Coriander is an annual herb, now widely available in supermarkets. However, if you like to grow your own herbs, it will be happy in the garden, or in a pot on the windowsill. It originated in Europe, where it was a favourite in Ancient Rome – and migrated eastward to India and South-east Asia, and it is a particular favourite in Thailand.

75 G (3 OZ) BUTTER
½ BUNCH SPRING ONIONS, CHOPPED
250 G (8 OZ) MUSHROOMS
2 TABLESPOONS FRESH CORIANDER
½ TEASPOON SALT
½ TEASPOON CHILLI POWDER
½ TEASPOON GARLIC POWDER
2 TABLESPOONS LEMON JUICE
300 ML (½ PINT) WATER
300 ML (½ PINT) FRESH SINGLE CREAM
TO GARNISH
A FEW SPRIGS FRESH CORIANDER
1 TABLESPOON FRESH CREAM
½ SMALL SPRING ONION, FINELY CHOPPED

Melt the butter in a saucepan over a low heat. Add the chopped spring onions and fry them for 2 minutes before adding the mushrooms, coriander, salt, chilli powder, garlic powder and lemon juice.

Continue to stir-fry for about 3 minutes, then pour in the water and fresh cream. Stir the mixture gently, taste and adjust the seasoning, if necessary.

Transfer the mixture to a food processor and blend until smooth, about 1 minute. Return the soup to the saucepan and bring to the boil.

Transfer to 4 individual serving bowls and serve, garnished with the coriander, fresh cream and spring onion.

Spicy Vegetarian Croquettes

These vegetable croquettes are very delicious! Try varying the vegetables you choose to put in them. Other root vegetables could be used, in season.

2 LARGE POTATOES, BOILED AND ROUGHLY MASHED

1 SMALL CARROT, BOILED AND DICED

25 G (1 OZ) PEAS, BOILED

50 G (2 OZ) CANNED SWEETCORN KERNELS

2 FRESH GREEN CHILLIES, CHOPPED

1 TABLESPOON CHOPPED FRESH CORIANDER

2 TEASPOONS MANGO POWDER

1 TEASPOON SALT

ABOUT 300 ML (½ PINT) CORN OIL

4 CURRY LEAVES

½ TEASPOON ONION SEEDS

½ TEASPOON MUSTARD SEEDS

2 EGGS, BEATEN

175 G (6 OZ) BREADCRUMBS

TO GARNISH

½ ICEBERG LETTUCE, SHREDDED

1 ONION, SLICED IN RINGS

1 TOMATO, SLICED

1 LIME, CUT IN WEDGES

In a large bowl, mix the mashed potatoes, diced carrot, peas, sweetcorn, chopped chillies, fresh coriander, mango powder and salt together.

Heat 1 tablespoon of the oil in a saucepan until hot. Lower the heat to medium and add the curry leaves, onion seeds and mustard seeds, letting them sizzle for 1 minute. Remove the saucepan from the heat, add the vegetable mixture, mixing thoroughly and set aside to cool.

When the mixture is cool, make about 12 croquettes. Dip them into the beaten eggs and then roll them in the breadcrumbs, coating them thoroughly. Set aside.

Heat the remaining oil in a karahi or deep frying pan and fry the croquettes in batches, using a slotted spoon to turn them frequently, until golden brown.

Remove from the pan with the slotted spoon and drain on absorbent kitchen paper.

Serve the croquettes garnished with the iceberg lettuce, onion rings, tomato slices and lime wedges.

Vegetable Pakoras

Pakoras are small pieces of vegetable, which are dipped in a marvellously light batter, made from besun or gram flour, then deep-fried. This is a delicious and simple dish – serve it as a starter accompanied by chutneys or dipping sauces, as finger-food with drinks, or as an accompaniment to other curry dishes.

4 TABLESPOONS GRAM FLOUR

2 TABLESPOONS PLAIN FLOUR

1½ TEASPOONS SALT

1 TEASPOON BICARBONATE OF SODA

1½ TEASPOONS CRUSHED DRIED RED CHILLIES

1 TEASPOON CRUSHED CORIANDER SEEDS

1 TEASPOON CRUSHED POMEGRANATE SEEDS

1 TEASPOON CRUSHED WHITE CUMIN SEEDS

¼ TEASPOON TURMERIC

3 TABLESPOONS CHOPPED FRESH CORIANDER

3–4 GREEN CHILLIES, CHOPPED

300 ML (½ PINT) WATER

1 ONION, SLICED

1 LARGE POTATO, CUT INTO STRIPS

8–10 FRESH SPINACH LEAVES

½ SMALL CAULIFLOWER, CUT INTO FLORETS

OIL FOR DEEP-FRYING

Sift the gram flour, plain flour, salt and bicarbonate of soda into a bowl. Add the spices, the chopped coriander and green chillies to the bowl, then gradually pour in the water, mixing it in with a fork to form a smooth batter.

Add the prepared vegetables to the batter. If it feels too stiff, pour in a little water to loosen the mixture.

Heat the oil in a karahi or deep frying pan and drop in about 1 tablespoon of batter at a time and deep-fry, turning once over a medium heat.

Remove each pakora with a slotted spoon once it is cooked and drain on absorbent kitchen paper. Repeat the process until all the batter is finished. This amount of mixture should make about 12–15 pakoras.

Serve the vegetable pakoras immediately with a spicy tomato sauce or a tamarind chutney.

RIGHT: *Two excellent recipes to serve as starters – at the top of the photograph are Vegetable Pakoras (recipe above, right) and below, Spicy Vegetarian Croquettes (recipe above). Both are equally good to serve at a drinks party, together with the Spicy Tomato Ketchup or Spicy Dip on page 117 or one of the Tamarind Chutneys on page 111.*

Panir and Vegetable Samosas

*These samosas make an excellent snack any time of the
day and can also be served as a starter with any
of the chutneys in this book.*

2 POTATOES, ROUGHLY DICED

1 CARROT, ROUGHLY DICED

300 ML (½ PINT) CORN OIL

1 SMALL ONION

¼ TEASPOON ONION SEEDS

50 G (2 OZ) FROZEN SWEETCORN KERNELS

50 G (2 OZ) FROZEN PEAS

125 G (4 OZ) PANIR (SEE PAGE 67), CUT INTO SMALL CUBES

1 TABLESPOON FINELY CHOPPED FRESH CORIANDER

2 RED CHILLIES, CHOPPED

1 TEASPOON CHILLI POWDER

1 TEASPOON MANGO POWDER

½ TEASPOON SALT

PASTRY

175 G (6 OZ) SELF-RAISING FLOUR

½ TEASPOON SALT

50 G (2 OZ) BUTTER, CUT INTO SMALL CUBES

6 TABLESPOONS WATER

Cook the potatoes and carrots in boiling salted water, until
cooked but not mushy. Drain and set aside.

Heat 3 tablespoons of the oil in a heavy-based saucepan
until hot and fry the onion and onion seeds for 2 minutes.
Lower the heat, add the potatoes, carrot, sweetcorn and peas
and lightly fry them for about 1 minute before adding the panir
cubes, coriander, chopped chillies, chilli powder, mango
powder and salt. Mix gently, remove the pan from the heat and
leave to cool.

Meanwhile, make the pastry. Sift the flour and salt into a
bowl. Add the butter and rub it into the flour, using your
fingertips until the mixture resembles breadcrumbs. Pour in
the water gradually, mixing it in with a fork. Pat the dough
into a ball and knead with the back of your hand for about
5 minutes or until the dough is smooth. Dust the dough with
a little flour, cover and set aside.

Break the dough into 5–6 balls and roll out very thinly into
circles. Cut in half, dampen the edges of each semi-circle and
shape them into cones. Fill the cones with a little of the cooled
vegetable filling, dampen the top and bottom of the edges and
pinch together to seal. Set aside.

Heat the remaining oil in a karahi or deep frying pan until
hot. Carefully lower the samosas into the oil a few at a time
and fry for 2–3 minutes or until golden brown, turning them
over at least once.

Remove the samosas from the oil with a slotted spoon and
drain on kitchen paper. They are best served immediately, but
may be reheated in a moderate oven or a microwave.

Spicy Diamond-shaped Pastry Bites
(Namak Paras)

*These are a delicious teatime snack – very easy to make,
and much, much more delicious than potato crisps. They are
very good as nibbles at a drinks party too. Although it is not
traditional, you could serve them with a dip, such as a dhaal
from the Pulses chapter. Also suitable would be one of the
chutneys or pickles from the Accompaniments chapter. Many
of these Indian snacks can be very spicy. If you find yourself
'overheated', never drink water, alcohol or soft drinks to cool
the fires – it simply doesn't work. Instead, try yogurt, rice,
bananas or coconut. Yogurt is cooling in dips, or in the
traditional drink, lassi (recipes on pages 26 and 120).*

175 G (6 OZ) SELF-RAISING FLOUR

1 TEASPOON SALT

50 G (2 OZ) UNSALTED BUTTER, CUT INTO SMALL CUBES

½ TEASPOON CRUSHED DRIED RED CHILLIES

½ TEASPOON WHITE CUMIN SEEDS

WATER

Sieve the flour and salt into a mixing bowl. Add the butter,
chillies and cumin seeds. Using your hands, blend together,
gradually pouring in sufficient water to form a soft dough.

Dust the dough with flour and knead it for 3–5 minutes. Let
the dough rest for 10–15 minutes.

Break the dough into two pieces and roll each piece out on a
lightly floured surface to a thickness of about 3 mm (⅛ inch).
Using a very sharp knife, cut the dough into 5 cm (2 inch)
diamond shapes.

Heat the oil in a karahi or deep frying pan to 180°C (350°F),
or until a cube of bread browns in 30 seconds, and fry the
pastry diamonds in batches, turning them once, until golden.
Remove them from the pan with a slotted spoon and drain on
absorbent kitchen paper.

Uppuma

Indian cooking is unbeatable for its huge range of snacks and savouries. Many of these are perfect for serving at drinks parties, although these parties were not, until recently, part of the largely-teetotal Indian way of life. A stroll down any Indian street will often produce an enormous variety of different foods available from street stalls. These range from delicious drinks of freshly-squeezed sugar-cane juice, to dozens of bite-sized treats such as those described in this chapter. Semolina is used to make various sweet dishes, and also this recipe for uppuma, which can be served as a savoury snack at any time of the day. Semolina is the hard part of the wheat grain, and is used to make couscous in North Africa, and pasta and puddings in Western cooking.

2 TABLESPOONS CHANA DHAAL
3 TABLESPOONS CORN OIL
1 TEASPOON MUSTARD SEEDS
8–10 CURRY LEAVES
1 TABLESPOON PEANUTS
1 TABLESPOON CASHEW NUTS
1½ TEASPOONS SALT
50 G (2 OZ) PEAS
175 G (6 OZ) COARSE SEMOLINA
½ TEASPOON DRIED RED CHILLIES, CRUSHED
600 ML (1 PINT) WATER
2 TABLESPOONS LEMON JUICE

Wash the chana dhaal, boil it until soft, drain and set aside.

Heat the oil in a large frying pan until hot and fry the mustard seeds and curry leaves for a few seconds.

Lower the heat and add the peanuts and cashew nuts, frying them quickly before adding the salt, peas, semolina, red chillies and the chana dhaal and stir-fry for about 1 minute.

Pour in the water and cook for about 3 minutes or until the water is fully absorbed.

Pour in the lemon juice and serve.

VARIATION

Uppuma with Urid Dhaal and Fresh Coriander
You could also substitute whole black urid dhaal for the chana dhaal, and add about 1 tablespoon of chopped, fresh coriander leaves to the mixture before stir-frying.

Fried Spicy Peas

Ideal to serve with drinks. The only problem is that these spicy peas disappear at an unbelievable rate, so for a large party I suggest you make multiple quantities. I find that frozen peas are not only easier to deal with, but their quality is more dependable.

500 G (1 LB) FROZEN PEAS, THAWED
300 ML (½ PINT) OIL FOR FRYING
1 TEASPOON CHILLI POWDER
½ TEASPOON GROUND CORIANDER
1 TEASPOON SALT
1 TEASPOON MANGO POWDER

Place the peas in a strainer to drain off any excess liquid.

Heat the oil in a heavy-based saucepan or karahi and fry the peas for 3–5 minutes. Remove from the pan with a slotted spoon and drain on absorbent kitchen paper.

Meanwhile, in a large mixing bowl, mix together the chilli powder, ground coriander, salt and mango powder. Put the peas in the bowl, hold a large plate on top and shake thoroughly so that the peas are well coated with the spices.

Stir-fried Cauliflower and Peas

A quick and easy dish to prepare, which can be served as an accompaniment to any lentil dish.

4 TABLESPOONS CORN OIL
1 ONION
½ TEASPOON BLACK CUMIN SEEDS
3 BLACK CARDAMOMS
6 BLACK PEPPERCORNS
1 x 2.5 CM (1 INCH) PIECE CINNAMON STICK
1 TEASPOON SALT
¼ TEASPOON TURMERIC
2 RED CHILLIES, SLICED
1 SMALL CAULIFLOWER, BROKEN INTO FLORETS
250 G (8 OZ) PEAS
2 TABLESPOONS CHOPPED FRESH CORIANDER
1 TABLESPOON LEMON JUICE

Heat the oil in a wide pan to 180°C (350°F), or until a cube of bread browns in 30 seconds, and fry the onion with the cumin seeds, cardamoms, black peppercorns and cinnamon for about 2 minutes. Stir in the salt, turmeric, red chillies, cauliflower florets and peas and continue to stir-fry for a further 5 minutes. Finally, add the fresh coriander and lemon juice and serve.

Curries

Many of your vegetarian meals may be planned
around splendidly varied, deliciously spicy recipes
in this chapter. There is a very wide choice of
curries, from simple combinations of one or two
lightly spiced vegetables, suitable for an everyday
family meal, and more elaborate dishes suitable
for an elegant dinner party.

Doodhi or Marrow with Moong Dhaal
(Kaddu Aur Moong Dhaal)

This curry goes particularly well with chapatis, and again marries doodhi with its 'soul mate', fenugreek.

1 BUNCH FRESH FENUGREEK

4 TABLESPOONS CORN OIL

2 ONIONS, DICED

½ TEASPOON MIXED FENUGREEK SEEDS AND ONION SEEDS

1 TEASPOON GROUND CUMIN

1 TEASPOON GARLIC PULP

¼ TEASPOON TURMERIC

1 TEASPOON CHILLI POWDER

750 G (1½ LB) DOODHI, OR MARROW, PEELED AND CUT INTO 2.5 CM (1 INCH) CUBES

1 TEASPOON SALT

50 G (2 OZ) MOONG DHAAL, WASHED AND DRAINED

1 TABLESPOON LEMON JUICE

Prepare the fenugreek by breaking off the leaves.

Heat the oil in a karahi or deep frying pan, add the onions, fenugreek seeds and onion seeds and fry until golden brown. Lower the heat and add the ground cumin, garlic, turmeric, chilli power, fenugreek leaves and doodhi or marrow cubes and stir-fry for about 3 minutes.

Add the salt, then the moong dhaal and lemon juice. Cover the pan and cook for 5–7 minutes over a very low heat, stirring occasionally, until the dhaal is cooked and the doodhi is soft.

VARIATIONS

Chayote with Moong Dhaal

Chayote, sometimes known as 'choko', is sold in Caribbean markets as 'chow-chow'. This small, pale green vegetable is also a variety of marrow and grows on a climbing vine. It is suitable for this recipe, as well as the one on the right, with fenugreek. Peel a similar quantity of chayotes and chop into 2.5 cm (1 inch) cubes – you don't have to remove the seeds; they have a lovely, nutty taste. Proceed as in the main recipe.

PREVIOUS PAGES: *From left, Stir-fried Baby Onions with Panir (recipe page 67) and Cauliflower in a Hot and Sour Sauce (recipe page 59). Panir is a very versatile Indian cheese, either crumbly like cottage cheese, or firm like soft Cheddar. It can be cut into cubes, cooked in clarified butter, and added to many dishes such as this one with baby onions.*

Doodhi or Marrow with Fenugreek
(Kaddu Aur Methi)

Doodhi is an Indian variety of marrow, also known as squash, and is available in Asian greengrocers. Ordinary marrows are a perfect substitute, and you will find that these methods of preparation make the rather bland flavour of marrow really come into its own. Baby patty-pan squash in green or yellow may also be used. Doodhi and fragrant fenugreek go very well together. In this recipe, stir-frying brings out the flavour of the fenugreek.

4 TABLESPOONS CORN OIL

½ TEASPOON MIXED WHITE CUMIN SEEDS AND FENUGREEK SEEDS

2 ONIONS, SLICED

¼ TEASPOON TURMERIC

1 TEASPOON CHILLI POWDER

1 TEASPOON SALT

750 G (1½ LB) DOODHI OR MARROW, PEELED AND CUT INTO 2.5 CM (1 INCH) CUBES

1 BUNCH FRESH FENUGREEK LEAVES

2 GREEN CHILLIES, CHOPPED

1 X 2.5 CM (1 INCH) PIECE FRESH GINGER, SHREDDED

Heat the oil in a saucepan, add the cumin and fenugreek seeds and stir-fry for about 1 minute, then add the sliced onions and continue frying for about 3 minutes. Lower the heat and stir in the turmeric, chilli powder and the salt.

Next add the doodhi or marrow pieces, fresh fenugreek leaves, and green chillies. Using a wooden spoon, stir-fry for about 2 minutes, then lower the heat further, cover the saucepan and cook for 5–7 minutes. Remove the lid and add the shredded ginger. Cook for a further 2 minutes.

Serve hot with puris.

VARIATIONS

Pumpkin with Fenugreek

Pumpkin is from the same botanical family as marrow, and can be happily adapted to this recipe. Substitute a similar quantity of peeled, deseeded and cubed pumpkin, and add 1 teaspoon of nutmeg at the same time as the chilli powder. Pumpkin and nutmeg have a special affinity for each other.

Courgettes with Fenugreek

Slice 750 g (1½ lb) courgettes into 2.5 cm (1 inch) pieces and proceed as in the main recipe. Do not peel the courgettes.

Vegetables Cooked with Bulgar Wheat
(Subzee Ka Haleem)

This is a recipe from the north of India – the wheat-growing region of the country. Bulgar wheat is also known as 'cracked wheat', and is available either roasted or plain. It is a popular ingredient in vegetarian cooking, in some home-made mueslis, and is the major component of the Lebanese salad, tabbouleh.

150 G (5 OZ) BULGAR (CRACKED) WHEAT

6 TABLESPOONS CORN OIL

2 ONIONS, DICED

½ TEASPOON BLACK CUMIN SEEDS

3 WHOLE GREEN CARDAMOMS

1 TEASPOON GARAM MASALA

1½ TEASPOONS GROUND CORIANDER

1½ TEASPOONS CHILLI POWDER

1 TEASPOON GARLIC PULP

1 TEASPOON GINGER PULP

1½ TEASPOONS SALT

¼ TEASPOON TURMERIC

1 X 1.5 CM (1 INCH) PIECE CINNAMON STICK

2 POTATOES, DICED

1 AUBERGINE, PEELED AND DICED

2 TOMATOES, SLICED

1 BUNCH FRESH FENUGREEK LEAVES

1 SMALL CAULIFLOWER, BROKEN INTO FLORETS

175 G (6 OZ) NATURAL YOGURT

3 GREEN CHILLIES, CHOPPED

2 TABLESPOONS CHOPPED FRESH CORIANDER

3 TABLESPOONS LEMON JUICE

TO GARNISH

4 TABLESPOONS GHEE

1 ONION, SLICED

2 X 2.5 CM (1 INCH) PIECES FRESH GINGER, SHREDDED

2 GREEN CHILLIES, CHOPPED

1 TABLESPOON CHOPPED FRESH CORIANDER

1 TABLESPOON CHOPPED FRESH MINT

1 LIME, CUT INTO WEDGES

Soak the cracked wheat in water, preferably overnight.

Heat the oil in a heavy-based saucepan, add the onions and fry until golden brown. Lower the heat and add all the spices, stirring continuously.

Next, add the prepared potatoes, aubergine, tomatoes, fenugreek leaves and cauliflower, mix together gently and stir-fry continuously for about 2 minutes.

Whisk the yogurt and pour into the pan, then add the chopped chillies, fresh coriander and lemon juice. Lower the heat further, cover the saucepan and cook for 5–7 minutes, stirring occasionally to prevent the vegetables sticking.

Drain the cracked wheat and add it to the vegetables in the saucepan, mixing it in thoroughly.

If the mixture (called a *haleem*) seems too thick, add about 150 ml (¼ pint) water to loosen the consistency.

Cook for about 1 minute, remove the pan from the heat and transfer to a serving dish. Keep the *haleem* warm while you prepare the garnish.

Heat the ghee in a frying pan and fry the sliced onion until crisp and golden brown. While it is still hot and sizzling, pour it over the top of the *haleem* and garnish with the shredded ginger, green chillies, fresh coriander and mint. Serve with lime wedges and the naan bread recipe below.

Naan

Most Indian breads, such as those found on pages 102-103, are unleavened. Naan is the exception, widely used with curries in order to mop up the delicious sauces. In India, it is also used as an eating utensil, to pick up pieces of food, rather like an edible spoon or pair of tongs. Naan would be most often served in the north of the country, where breads are the basis of most meals. In the south, rice is the staple food, and a meal would be unthinkable without it. Naan is usually cooked in a tandoor oven, which produces a fierce heat. It would be impossible to replicate that heat in an ordinary domestic oven, and this recipe uses the grill instead. There are many naan bread recipes, but this is one is easy to follow.

1 TEASPOON SUGAR

1 TEASPOON FRESH YEAST

150 ML (¼ PINT) WARM WATER

250 G (8 OZ) PLAIN FLOUR

1 TABLESPOON GHEE

1 TEASPOON SALT

50 G (2 OZ) UNSALTED BUTTER

1 TEASPOON POPPY SEEDS

Dissolve the sugar and yeast in a cup with the warm water, then set aside for 10 minutes or until the mixture is frothy.

Place the flour in a large mixing bowl, make a well in the centre, add ghee, salt and yeast mixture. Mix well with your fingers, adding more water if required.

Knead on a floured surface for about 5 minutes or until smooth. Place the dough back in the bowl, cover and leave to rise in a warm place for 1½ hours or until doubled in size. Turn on to a floured surface and knead for a further 2 minutes.

Break off small balls and pat into rounds about 12 cm (5 inches) in diameter and 1 cm (½ inch) thick. Place on a greased sheet of foil and place under a very hot grill for 7–10 minutes, turning twice to brush with butter and sprinkle with poppy seeds. Serve immediately or wrap in foil until required.

Tomato Kadi
(Tamatar Ki Kadi)

*Kadi, a dish from South India, is probably also the word
from which 'curry' is derived.*

175 G (6 OZ) RED TAMARIND PASTE

300 ML (½ PINT) WATER

3 TABLESPOONS CORN OIL

1 ONION, DICED

1 TEASPOON GINGER PULP

1 TEASPOON GARLIC PULP

1 TEASPOON GROUND CUMIN

¼ TEASPOON TURMERIC

1 TEASPOON CHILLI POWDER

1 TEASPOON SALT

1 TEASPOON GROUND CORIANDER

3 TOMATOES, QUARTERED

2 TABLESPOONS GROUND RICE

2 TABLESPOONS CHOPPED FRESH CORIANDER

FOR THE BAGHAAR

3 TABLESPOONS OIL

½ TEASPOON WHITE CUMIN SEEDS

3 DRIED RED CHILLIES

6 CURRY LEAVES

TO GARNISH

FRESH CORIANDER

GREEN CHILLIES

Soak the tamarind paste in hot water to cover for about
15–20 minutes. Squeeze the softened tamarind with your hand
to extract as much pulp as possible and push it through a
sieve. Pour the measured water on to the pulp to loosen it
and then set aside.

Meanwhile, heat the oil in a saucepan over a medium heat
and fry the onion until golden brown. Lower the heat and
gradually stir in the ginger, garlic, cumin, turmeric, chilli
powder, salt, ground coriander and the tamarind pulp. Increase
the heat, add the tomatoes and bring to the boil. Then lower
the heat and slowly stir in the ground rice, a little at a time,
stirring continuously. Add the fresh coriander and cook slowly
for 3–5 minutes. Remove the pan from the heat and set aside.

Prepare the baghaar; heat the oil in a frying pan and fry the
cumin seeds, red chillies and curry leaves until they turn a
shade darker. Pour over the kadi while still sizzling.

Serve garnished with fresh coriander and green chillies.

Vegetable Jalfrezi
(Subzee Ki Jalfrezi)

*Though panir is not generally used in this hot and spicy
dish, I find that it enhances the flavour of the curry – and, of
course, panir is a very good source of protein.*

4 TABLESPOONS CORN OIL

½ TEASPOON MIXED ONION SEEDS, MUSTARD SEEDS AND
FENUGREEK SEEDS

4 CURRY LEAVES

2 TABLESPOONS TOMATO PURÉE

1 TEASPOON GROUND CUMIN

1½ TEASPOONS GROUND CORIANDER

1 TEASPOON GINGER PULP

1 TEASPOON GARLIC PULP

1 TEASPOON CHILLI POWDER

2 TEASPOONS SALT

2 TEASPOONS MANGO POWDER

300ML (½ PINT) WATER

VEGETABLES

3 TOMATOES, CUT INTO WEDGES

½ GREEN PEPPER, DESEEDED AND SLICED

½ RED PEPPER, DESEEDED AND SLICED

1 LARGE CARROT

75 G (3 OZ) GREEN BEANS

125 G (4 OZ) PANIR

2 GREEN CHILLIES, DESEEDED AND SLICED

2 TABLESPOONS FRESH CORIANDER

150 ML (¼ PINT) WATER

Heat the oil in a heavy-based saucepan, add all the whole
seeds and curry leaves and fry them until they change colour.
Remove the pan from the heat and set aside.

Mix the tomato purée, all the spices and water together and
pour into the saucepan containing the oil, seeds and curry
leaves. Return to the heat and cook for about 2 minutes.

Gradually add the vegetables, panir and the green chillies to
the pan, stirring to coat with the spiced oil.

Add the fresh coriander and water, cover the pan and cook
over a very low heat until all the vegetables are cooked.

Serve the curry hot with rice or chapatis.

RIGHT: *From top: Tomato Kadi (recipe above) and Vegetable Jalfrezi
(recipe above right).*

Vegetables in a Tangy Sauce

(Khutti Meethi Subzee)

This sauce is packed with flavour – feel free to substitute other vegetables in season for the ones listed here. Cauliflowers, courgettes and marrow would also be delicious in this recipe.

75 G (3 OZ) TOOR DHAAL

300 ML (½ PINT) WATER

2 TABLESPOONS GREEK YOGURT

1 TABLESPOON TOMATO PURÉE

2 TEASPOONS RED TAMARIND PASTE

150 ML (¼ PINT) WATER

1 TEASPOON GINGER PULP

1 TEASPOON GARLIC PULP

1½ TEASPOONS CHILLI POWDER

½ TEASPOON SUGAR

1 TEASPOON SALT

1 TEASPOON GROUND CUMIN

1 TEASPOON GROUND CORIANDER

3 TABLESPOONS CORN OIL

4 WHOLE CURRY LEAVES

½ TEASPOON ONION SEEDS

4 WHOLE DRIED RED CHILLIES

½ TEASPOON WHITE CUMIN SEEDS

12–14 BABY ONIONS, PEELED

12 BABY POTATOES, HALVED AND BOILED

12–14 CHERRY TOMATOES

2 CARROTS, THICKLY SLICED

75 ML (3 FL OZ) SINGLE CREAM

2 TABLESPOONS CHOPPED FRESH CORIANDER

3 GREEN CHILLIES

Boil the toor dhaal in the 300 ml (½ pint) water until soft but not mushy and set aside.

Mix together the yogurt, tomato purée, tamarind paste, the 150 ml (¼ pint) water, ginger, garlic, chilli powder, sugar, salt, cumin and coriander together in bowl and set aside.

Heat the oil in a karahi or deep frying pan, add the curry leaves, onion seeds, dried red chillies and cumin seeds and fry over a medium heat until they are a shade darker. Add the whole baby onions and stir-fry them until they are browned all over. Add the baby potatoes, cherry tomatoes and carrots, and stir-fry continuously. Pour in the yogurt mixture and cook for 2 minutes, then stir in the cream.

Finally, mix in the fresh coriander and green chillies and serve the vegetables hot.

Illustrated on page 95.

Vegetables in a Rich Creamy Sauce

150 G (5 OZ) GREEK YOGURT

1 TABLESPOON TOMATO PURÉE

2 TABLESPOONS LEMON JUICE

1 TEASPOON GINGER PULP

1 TEASPOON GARLIC PULP

1 TEASPOON CHILLI POWDER

1 TEASPOON SALT

1 TEASPOON GROUND CORIANDER

1 TEASPOON GROUND CUMIN

2 TABLESPOONS GROUND ALMONDS

150 ML (¼ PINT) WATER

75 G (3 OZ) UNSALTED BUTTER

4 TABLESPOONS CORN OIL

½ TEASPOON MIXED ONION SEEDS AND MUSTARD SEEDS

6 SMALL THICK GREEN CHILLIES, SLIT DOWN THE CENTRE AND DESEEDED

8–10 CAULIFLOWER FLORETS

4–5 BABY POTATOES, THICKLY SLICED

1 CARROT, SLICED

5 BABY ONIONS, PEELED

8–10 PANIR CUBES

300 ML (½ PINT) WATER

175 ML (6 FL OZ) SINGLE CREAM

2 TABLESPOONS CHOPPED FRESH CORIANDER

2 GREEN CHILLIES, CHOPPED

50 G (2 OZ) FLAKED ALMONDS, TO GARNISH

Blend the yogurt, tomato purée, lemon juice, ginger, garlic, chilli powder, salt, coriander, cumin, ground almonds and water in a medium-size mixing bowl and set aside.

Heat the unsalted butter and oil in a karahi or deep frying pan. Add the onion and mustard seeds and fry until they turn a shade darker. Fry the vegetables, one kind at a time, in the oil until they are cooked, starting with the green chillies then the cauliflower, potatoes, carrot, and whole baby onions, and ending with the panir cubes. Remove the fried vegetables from the pan with a slotted spoon, and drain on kitchen paper.

Add the spice and yogurt mixture to the remaining butter and oil in the pan. Pour in the measured water and cook for about 5 minutes, until the sauce comes to the boil. Return the fried vegetables to the pan, stirring gently to mix the vegetables and sauce together, without breaking them.

Finally, pour in the cream, fresh coriander and green chillies and cook for 3–5 minutes.

Serve garnished with the flaked almonds.

Cauliflower in a Creamy Sauce

Cauliflower seems to be particularly suited to creamy sauces, but you could also substitute other vegetables in this curry.

1 TEASPOON GROUND CORIANDER
2 TEASPOONS GROUND ALMONDS
2 ONIONS, ROUGHLY CHOPPED
1 TEASPOON GARLIC PULP
1 TEASPOON GINGER PULP
1 TEASPOON SALT
3 GREEN CHILLIES, ROUGHLY CHOPPED
2 TABLESPOONS CHOPPED FRESH CORIANDER
1 TABLESPOON CORN OIL
75 G (3 OZ) BUTTER
4 CURRY LEAVES
½ CAULIFLOWER, CUT INTO SMALL FLORETS
½ GREEN PEPPER, DESEEDED AND DICED
½ RED PEPPER, DESEEDED AND DICED
175 ML (6 FL OZ) SINGLE CREAM

Blend the ground coriander, ground almonds, onions, garlic, ginger, salt, 2 of the chopped green chillies and 1 tablespoon of the chopped fresh coriander in a food processor for 1 minute or until the mixture is fairly smooth.

Heat the oil and butter together in a heavy-based saucepan, add the curry leaves and fry until they are a shade darker.

Pour the spice and onion mixture into the pan and stir-fry over a medium heat for about 3 minutes, or until the onion mixture is cooked.

Add the cauliflower florets and continue to stir-fry the contents of the pan for a further 2 minutes.

Then add the green and red peppers, the remaining chopped fresh coriander and chopped green chilli as well as the cream. Cook through for 2 minutes and serve hot with puris (see recipe on page 102).

Shahi Panir Koftas

This curry has a delicious and creamy sauce. Served with freshly made masala puri (see recipe on page 102), it makes an excellent meal. Panir, a very good source of protein, is eaten all over India. Though available in Asian grocers, the homemade variety is best for this recipe. There is another recipe for preparing panir on page 67.

PANIR
1.2 LITRES (2 PINTS) FULL CREAM MILK
2 TABLESPOONS LEMON JUICE
SHAHI PANIR KOFTA SAUCE
75 G (3 OZ) BUTTER
1 TABLESPOON CORN OIL
1 CINNAMON STICK
2 GREEN CARDAMOMS
3 TABLESPOONS NATURAL YOGURT
3 TABLESPOONS TOMATO PURÉE
1 TEASPOON GARAM MASALA
1 TEASPOON CHILLI POWDER
¼ TEASPOON TURMERIC
1 TEASPOON GROUND CORIANDER
1 TEASPOON SALT
1 TABLESPOON LEMON JUICE
150 ML (¼ PINT) WATER
2 TABLESPOONS CHOPPED FRESH CORIANDER
2 GREEN CHILLIES, CHOPPED
200 ML (7 FL OZ) SINGLE CREAM

First, make the panir. Bring the milk slowly to the boil over a medium heat then add the lemon juice, stirring continuously. The milk will now begin to thicken and curdle. Wait until all the liquid (the whey) has evaporated and you are left with the curdled milk (the curds).

Strain the curdled milk through a sieve and press down to get rid of any excess liquid. When cool, divide the mixture into 8–10 spoonfuls and mould them into small round balls, a little smaller than a golf ball, making sure they look smooth. Set the panir balls aside on a plate in the refrigerator.

For the sauce, heat the butter and oil in a medium-sized saucepan. When the butter has melted, add the cinnamon stick and the cardamoms and fry for a few seconds. Remove the pan from the heat and set aside.

Mix together the yogurt, tomato purée, garam masala, chilli powder, turmeric, ground coriander, salt, lemon juice and water together in bowl.

Return the saucepan to the heat, pour in the yogurt mixture and fry over a medium/low heat. Drop the koftas into the sauce, followed by the fresh coriander, chillies and cream and mix gently together, stirring continuously. Cook for a further 5 minutes, or until the sauce has thickened. Serve hot.

Mixed Vegetables in a Butter Sauce
(Mili Huwi Subzee Makhan Ki Sauce May)

This is sure to be a favourite with your family and friends. It has a rich sauce and is full of flavour.

75 G (3 OZ) GREEK YOGURT

1 TABLESPOON TOMATO PURÉE

½ TEASPOON GARAM MASALA

1 TEASPOON GINGER PULP

1 TEASPOON CHILLI POWDER

¼ TEASPOON GROUND CARDAMOMS

1 TEASPOON GARLIC PULP

1 TEASPOON GROUND CORIANDER

1 TEASPOON SALT

¼ TEASPOON COARSELY GROUND BLACK PEPPER

75 G (3 OZ) BUTTER

1 TABLESPOON CORN OIL

2 ONIONS, DICED

2 BAY LEAVES

2 PIECES CINNAMON BARK

2 POTATOES, ROUGHLY DICED

1 LARGE CARROT, SLICED

50 G (2 OZ) GREEN BEANS, SLICED

½ CAULIFLOWER, CUT INTO SMALL FLORETS

2 FRESH GREEN CHILLIES, CHOPPED

2 TABLESPOONS CHOPPED FRESH CORIANDER

300 ML (½ PINT) WATER

150 ML (¼ PINT) SINGLE CREAM

Mix the yogurt, tomato purée, garam masala, ginger, chilli powder, cardamoms, garlic pulp, coriander, salt and pepper in a medium-size bowl and set aside.

Heat the butter and oil in a karahi or deep frying pan, add the onions, bay leaves and cinnamon bark and fry until the onions are golden brown. Pour the yogurt and spice mixture into the pan and stir-fry for about 1 minute.

Reduce the heat to low and let the spices cook slowly while preparing the vegetables.

Gradually stir the potatoes, carrot, beans, cauliflower, green chillies, and coriander into the pan. Add the water. Cook over a low heat until the vegetables are tender, but still firm enough to retain their shape and texture.

Pour in the cream and heat the dish to boiling point. Serve it with any of the rice dishes in this book.

Potatoes and Aubergines Cooked in Whole Spices
(Aloo Baigun Aur Sabuth Masalay)

Potatoes were not introduced to India until the 16th Century – probably by the Portuguese. Aubergines, however, are native to the sub-continent, and spread from there to almost every corner of the world. They are now particular favourites in all the countries around the Mediterranean. The two vegetables are delicious culinary partners in this dish – but it is important to choose small aubergines for this recipe.

4 TABLESPOONS CHOPPED FRESH CORIANDER

2 TABLESPOONS CHOPPED FRESH MINT

5 GREEN CHILLIES

2 BUNCHES SPRING ONIONS, CHOPPED

4 TABLESPOONS CORN OIL

½ TEASPOON ONION SEEDS

4 CURRY LEAVES

4 GARLIC CLOVES

1 X 2.5 CM (1 INCH) PIECE FRESH GINGER, SHREDDED

1 TEASPOON SALT

2 POTATOES, ROUGHLY CUBED

4 SMALL AUBERGINES, ROUGHLY CUBED

150 ML (¼ PINT) WATER

Place 3 tablespoons of the chopped fresh coriander, the mint, 2 of the green chillies, chopped, and spring onions in a food processor and grind them for about 1 minute.

Heat the oil in a saucepan, add the onion seeds, curry leaves, garlic and shredded ginger and fry for about 1 minute. Add the ground mixture from the processor to the pan, lower the heat and stir-fry for about 2 minutes. Add the potatoes and aubergines, mix together and pour in the measured water. Cover the saucepan with a tight-fitting lid and cook gently for 12–15 minutes.

When the vegetables are cooked, add the remaining chopped fresh coriander and the remaining 2 whole green chillies, and cook, stir-frying, for a further 2 minutes before serving.

OPPOSITE: *Mixed Vegetables in a Butter Sauce (recipe above, left), served with Aromatic Rice (recipe on page 92). Both dishes would be suitable for inclusion in a thali (recipe on page 75), the traditional Indian vegetarian meal. The thali is particularly associated with the largely-vegetarian south of India, but is now found all over the sub-continent, in the simplest village home and the grandest restaurants.*

Potatoes and Green Beans in a Coconut Sauce
(Aloo Phalli)

This mild curry with a thick creamy sauce comes from the coconut-growing south of India. It is delicious served with plain boiled rice.

250 G (8 OZ) NATURAL YOGURT

50 G (2 OZ) CREAMED COCONUT

1½ TEASPOONS GARAM MASALA

1 TEASPOON CHILLI POWDER

1 TEASPOON GINGER PULP

1 TEASPOON GARLIC PULP

¼ TEASPOON TURMERIC

¼ TEASPOON BLACK CUMIN SEEDS

¼ TEASPOON GROUND CARDAMOM

1 TEASPOON SALT

50 G (2 OZ) BUTTER

2 TABLESPOONS OIL

2 ONIONS, FINELY DICED

2 POTATOES, CUT IN 1 CM (½ INCH) DICE

75 G (3 OZ) GREEN BEANS

½ CAULIFLOWER, CUT INTO SMALL FLORETS

½ RED PEPPER, DESEEDED AND DICED

1 TABLESPOON CHOPPED FRESH CORIANDER

3 TABLESPOONS SINGLE CREAM

Whisk the yogurt together with the creamed coconut, garam masala, chilli powder, ginger, garlic, turmeric, cumin seeds, cardamom and salt.

Heat the butter and oil in a heavy-based saucepan, add the onions and stir-fry until browned. Pour in the yogurt mixture and stir-fry, for a further 2 minutes.

Lower the heat and add the remaining ingredients. Cover the pan and cook until the vegetables are soft but not mushy.

VARIATION
Okra, Tomatoes and Potatoes in a Coconut Sauce
Substitute 250 g (8 oz) fresh young okra, 3 medium-sized potatoes and 2 tomatoes for the potatoes and green beans in the main recipe. Rinse the okra and pat dry. Peel the potatoes and cut into large dice.

Proceed as in the main recipe, adding the tomatoes, cut into quarters, towards the end of the cooking time.

Potatoes with Sesame Seeds
(Aloo Thill)

Sesame seeds – widely used in Indian and Chinese cooking – have a delicious, sweet, nutty flavour. Look for the unhulled seeds in shops which stock a wide variety of Asian spices, rather than the common, hulled, creamy-coloured ones – you will really notice the difference in taste.

3 POTATOES, ROUGHLY DICED

4 TABLESPOONS OIL

1 ONION, DICED

1 TEASPOON WHITE CUMIN SEEDS

¼ TEASPOON TURMERIC

1 TEASPOON CHILLI POWDER

1 X 2.5 CM (1 INCH) PIECE FRESH GINGER, SHREDDED

1 TEASPOON SALT

2 FRESH RED CHILLIES, CHOPPED

1 TABLESPOON CHOPPED FRESH CORIANDER

2 TABLESPOONS SESAME SEEDS

Cook the potato dice in lightly salted water until soft. Drain and set aside.

Heat the oil in a karahi or deep frying pan, add the onion and cumin seeds and fry until the onions are lightly browned.

Lower the heat, mix in the turmeric, chilli powder, ginger and salt and mix in well. Add the cooked potatoes and stir-fry for about 2 minutes.

Add the red chillies, fresh coriander and sesame seeds and stir to mix well. Serve hot with naan (recipe on page 34) or chapatis (recipe on page 102).

Aloo Gobi

Literally, 'potatoes and cauliflower' – two favourite vegetarian ingredients. This is a dry vegetable curry which is delicious when served with any of the wet dhaal recipes from the Pulses chapter on pages 76–89.

5 TABLESPOONS CORN OIL

1 TEASPOON WHITE CUMIN SEEDS

4 WHOLE DRIED RED CHILLIES

1 PINCH ASAFOETIDA

1 TABLESPOON SHREDDED FRESH GINGER

3 GARLIC CLOVES

2 POTATOES, ROUGHLY DICED

1 SMALL CAULIFLOWER, CUT INTO SMALL FLORETS

1 TEASPOON SALT

2 FRESH RED CHILLIES, CHOPPED

1 TABLESPOON CHOPPED FRESH CORIANDER

1 TABLESPOON LEMON JUICE

2 TOMATOES, QUARTERED

Heat the oil in a heavy-based saucepan and fry the cumin seeds, the dried red chillies and asafoetida for a few seconds. Lower the heat and add the ginger and garlic cloves. Cook for about 20 seconds then add the potatoes and stir-fry on the lowered heat for about 3 minutes.

Next, add the cauliflower florets and continue to gently stir-fry for a further 2 minutes.

Stir in the salt, red chillies, coriander, lemon juice and tomatoes. Cover the pan and cook over a very low heat for 12–15 minutes, stirring very gently occasionally to ensure even cooking. Serve the Aloo Gobi hot.

VARIATION

Pumpkin and Broccoli Curry

Pumpkin and broccoli make an interesting and colourful variation for this recipe. Just remember that pumpkin cooks much faster than potatoes and broccoli cooks faster than cauliflower. Follow the main recipe, but cook for only 8–10 minutes, or until the pumpkin is tender.

Potato and Pea Korma
(Aloo Matar Ka Korma)

Korma dishes, a legacy of the Moghul's rule in India, are very popular with Westerners who are new to very spicy food, since they are mild and creamy. So – if you are having guests who might be a little wary of a very hot curry, serve a korma, and they will love it! This one has a delicious and thick sauce and should be served with paratas.

2 TEASPOONS POPPY SEEDS

2 TEASPOONS SESAME SEEDS

6 TABLESPOONS NATURAL YOGURT

1 TEASPOON GARAM MASALA

1 TEASPOON GINGER PULP

1½ TEASPOONS GROUND CORIANDER

1 TEASPOON GARLIC PULP

1 TEASPOON CHILLI POWDER

1 TEASPOON SALT

1 TABLESPOON LEMON JUICE

1 TABLESPOON TOMATO PURÉE

5 TABLESPOONS MELTED BUTTER

1 TABLESPOON CORN OIL

2 WHOLE GREEN CARDAMOMS

4–6 BLACK PEPPERCORNS

1 X 2.5 CM (1 INCH) PIECE CINNAMON BARK, HALVED

2 ONIONS

10 BABY POTATOES

50 G (2 OZ) FROZEN GREEN BEANS

50 G (2 OZ) FROZEN PEAS

2 TOMATOES, QUARTERED

1 TEASPOON CHOPPED FRESH CORIANDER

1 TEASPOON FRESH MINT

SINGLE CREAM

First, dry-roast the poppy seeds and sesame seeds (see page 8). When cool, place the seeds in a spice grinder and grind to a powder. Remove from the grinder and place in a bowl.

Add the yogurt, garam masala, ginger, ground coriander, garlic, chilli powder, salt, lemon juice and tomato purée. Using a whisk, blend together and set aside.

Heat the butter with the corn oil in a heavy-based saucepan and drop in the cardamoms, peppercorns and cinnamon bark. Next, add the onions and fry until they are golden brown.

Pour in the yogurt and spice mixture and stir-fry for about 2 minutes over a low heat.

Add the potatoes, beans and peas and stir.

If the mixture seems too dry, add 150 ml (¼ pint) water. Cover the pan and cook until the vegetables are cooked.

Add the tomato quarters, fresh coriander, fresh mint and stir in the cream. Cook for a further 2 minutes, then serve hot.

Onion Bhajias and Vegetables in a Yogurt and Gram Flour Sauce

(Dahl Ki Kadi)

Bhajias are a favourite Indian dish in the West. They can be served as a main dish, as here, or simply as a starter. You will find recipes for Mushroom and Leek Bhajias and plain Onion Bhajias in the Starters and Snacks chapter on page 21. India boasts a wide selection of snack foods, and bhajias are perhaps the most widely-known of all these.

125 G (4 OZ) GRAM FLOUR

1½ TEASPOONS CHILLI POWDER

1 TEASPOON SALT

½ TEASPOON BICARBONATE OF SODA

1 ONION, SLICED

2 GREEN CHILLIES

1 TABLESPOON CHOPPED FRESH CORIANDER

150 ML (¼ PINT) WATER

ABOUT 300 ML (½ PINT) CORN OIL

YOGURT GRAM FLOUR SAUCE

300 ML (½ PINT) NATURAL YOGURT

2 TABLESPOONS GRAM FLOUR

300 ML (½ PINT) WATER

1 TEASPOON GINGER PULP

1 TEASPOON GARLIC PULP

1 TEASPOON CHILLI POWDER

1½ TEASPOONS SALT

½ TEASPOON TURMERIC

1 TEASPOON GROUND CORIANDER

1 TEASPOON GROUND CUMIN

1 COURGETTE, SLICED

6 SMALL CAULIFLOWER FLORETS

1 SMALL RED PEPPER,
DESEEDED AND COARSELY DICED

2 GREEN CHILLIES, CHOPPED

300 ML (½ PINT) CORN OIL

BAGHAAR TARICA

3 TABLESPOONS CORN OIL

4 CURRY LEAVES

1 TEASPOON MIXED ONION SEEDS,
MUSTARD SEEDS AND WHITE CUMIN SEEDS

3 DRIED RED CHILLIES

2 TABLESPOONS CHOPPED FRESH CORIANDER,
TO GARNISH

To make the bhajia batter, mix the gram flour, chilli powder, salt, bicarbonate of soda, onion slices, green chillies, fresh coriander and water together in a medium-size bowl.

Prepare the yogurt gram flour sauce; in a large bowl, whisk the yogurt with the gram flour and water, and then add the ginger and garlic and all the spices. Pour the mixture through a sieve into a medium-sized saucepan, place over a low heat and bring to the boil, stirring occasionally and adding a little extra water, if the sauce gets too thick. Gradually add the courgette, cauliflower, red pepper and green chillies and continue to cook over a low heat until the vegetables are cooked. Transfer to a serving dish and set aside.

To make the bhajias, heat the corn oil in a karahi or a deep frying pan to 180°C (350°F), or until a cube of bread browns in 30 seconds. Start frying the gram flour batter, dropping about a tablespoon at a time into the hot oil and turning it at least twice. Fry over a medium heat until they turn a golden brown. Remove the bhajias from the oil with a slotted spoon, and place them on top of the yogurt gram flour sauce.

To make the baghaar tarica, heat the oil in a small saucepan until it is quite hot and then add the curry leaves, onion seeds, mustard seeds, white cumin seeds and dried red chillies; within 30 seconds they should turn a shade darker. Remove the saucepan from the heat and pour the baghaar tarica over the bhajias and sauce.

Garnish the dish with chopped fresh coriander and serve immediately with plain boiled rice and a knob of butter.

RIGHT: *Bhajias are one of the best-known Indian snack foods. However, this dish of Onion Bhajias and Vegetables in a Yogurt and Gram Flour Sauce (recipe above), served with plain boiled rice, makes the bhajia into a much more substantial main-course dish.*

Buttered Saag
(Makhani Saag)

Try to use fresh young spinach leaves for this recipe, as it really helps to improve the flavour. However, if this is not available, frozen leaf spinach will do. This is perhaps the simplest and easiest way to serve spinach in an Indian menu. Use good, unsalted butter, and clarify it to form ghee, if you wish. This will stop the butter from burning quite so easily. To clarify butter, place it in a saucepan and bring it to the boil. It will separate into golden butter and whitish milk solids. Pour off the clarified butter, leaving the milk solids behind.

1 KG (2 LB) YOUNG SPINACH LEAVES
150 G (5 OZ) BUTTER
1 LARGE ONION, DICED
1 X 2.5 CM (1 INCH) PIECE FRESH GINGER, SHREDDED
3 GARLIC CLOVES, SLICED
¼ TEASPOON TURMERIC
1 TEASPOON CHILLI POWDER
1 TEASPOON GARAM MASALA
1 BUNCH FRESH CORIANDER, CHOPPED
2 TABLESPOONS LEMON JUICE
TO GARNISH
2 RED CHILLIES, SLICED
1 X 2.5 CM (1 INCH) PIECE FRESH GINGER, SHREDDED
1 TOMATO, DESEEDED AND DICED
50 G (2 OZ) KNOB OF BUTTER

Wash the spinach leaves thoroughly and roughly chop. Cook the spinach in the water left on the leaves until soft. Drain, squeeze out any excess water and set aside.

Melt the butter in a karahi or deep frying pan over a medium heat and gently fry the onion until soft with the ginger, garlic, turmeric, chilli powder and garam masala. Add the spinach and stir-fry for about 5 minutes.

Add the fresh coriander and mix it into the spinach, stirring continuously over a low heat. Then pour in the lemon juice. Transfer to a warmed serving dish and serve garnished with the red chillies, ginger, diced tomato and knob of butter.

Saag with Toor Dhaal

Saag, or spinach, is cooked with tomatoes in many different cuisines. Certainly their flavours go well together, but perhaps it's their colours which are so attractive. The red and green is repeated in the garnish of red chillies and fresh green coriander.
This dish may also be made using chana dhaal, instead of the toor dhaal.

500 G (1 LB) FRESH SPINACH LEAVES, BLANCHED
AND ROUGHLY CHOPPED
50 G (2 OZ) TOOR DHAAL
4 TABLESPOONS CORN OIL
1 X 425 G (14 OZ) CAN TOMATOES
1 TEASPOON GINGER PULP
1 TEASPOON GARLIC PULP
1½ TEASPOONS GROUND CORIANDER
1 TEASPOON GROUND CUMIN
1 TEASPOON CHILLI POWDER
2 TABLESPOONS LEMON JUICE
2 RED CHILLIES, CHOPPED
2 TABLESPOONS CHOPPED FRESH CORIANDER

Blanch the spinach in boiling water for about 3 minutes. Drain and squeeze out any excess liquid and set aside.

Wash the toor dhaal and cook in lightly salted boiling water until soft but not mushy. Drain and set aside.

Heat the oil in a karahi or a deep frying pan over a low heat and while it is heating mix the tomatoes and their juice, ginger, garlic, coriander, ground cumin, chilli powder and lemon juice together in a bowl. Pour the mixture into the oil and fry for at least 5–7 minutes.

Once the sauce has thickened add the spinach and cook, stirring occasionally, for 5–7 minutes.

Pour in the toor dhaal, the red chillies and fresh coriander. Serve hot with rice or chapatis.

Methi and Spinach Panir

Fenugreek, known as 'methi' in India, is available in some Asian greengrocers, but is not difficult to grow yourself. It is a plant which originated in the Middle East, and is used in cooking there, in North Africa and India. The leaves have a very strong scent, and are used either fresh (as here), or dried, as a vegetable or herb. The seeds are also used – they are slightly bitter until roasted or fried gently in hot oil. They smell rather like celery. Panir, the delicious Indian cooking cheese, can be bought at specialist shops, or you can make it yourself from the recipe on page 67.

175 G (6 OZ) PANIR

5 TABLESPOONS CORN OIL

50 G (2 OZ) BUTTER

1 POTATO, CUT INTO CHIPS

A LARGE BUNCH OF FRESH FENUGREEK LEAVES

250 G (8 OZ) FROZEN SPINACH

1 TEASPOON GINGER PULP

1 TEASPOON SALT

1 TEASPOON GROUND CORIANDER

¼ TEASPOON TURMERIC

1 TEASPOON CHILLI POWDER

2 TABLESPOONS CHOPPED FRESH CORIANDER,

2 RED CHILLIES, CHOPPED

75 G (3 OZ) NATURAL YOGURT

75 G (3 OZ) SWEETCORN KERNELS

Cut the panir into cubes. Heat the oil and the butter together in a heavy-based saucepan or a frying pan with a lid, add the cubes of panir, and fry until they are slightly golden. Remove them from the pan with a slotted spoon and drain on kitchen paper. Set aside.

Add the potato chips to the saucepan and fry until they are lightly golden. Remove from the oil and set aside on kitchen paper to drain.

Wash and drain the fenugreek leaves, then add them to the pan, together with the spinach, and fry for about 2 minutes before adding the ginger, salt, coriander, turmeric, chilli powder and fresh coriander. Reduce the heat and continue to stir-fry for about 3 minutes until all the spices are cooked.

Add the red chillies and stir in the yogurt and sweetcorn.

Continue to stir-fry gently until the yogurt has been absorbed into the spinach.

Finally, add the panir cubes and potatoes. Cover and cook for 5-7 minutes. Serve hot with boiled rice.

Tinday Methi with Moong Dhaal

Tinday is a vegetable very similar to doodhi (kaddu) in texture and flavour – and you could also substitute squash, marrow or even courgettes. If you are unable to find the fresh vegetable in an Asian greengrocer, canned tinday are widely available in Asian delicatessens, and are equally good. If you are using canned tinday, drain off the liquid first.

1 BUNCH FRESH FENUGREEK LEAVES

2 TABLESPOONS MOONG DHAAL, WASHED

4 TABLESPOONS CORN OIL

2 ONIONS, FINELY DICED

¼ TEASPOON ONION SEEDS

4 - 6 CURRY LEAVES

3 TOMATOES, DICED

1 TEASPOON GINGER PULP

1 TEASPOON GARLIC PULP

1½ TEASPOONS CHILLI POWDER

¼ TEASPOON GROUND FENNEL

1 TEASPOON SALT

500 G (1 LB) TINDAY, PEELED AND DICED

150 ML (¼ PINT) WATER (SEE METHOD)

3 GREEN CHILLIES, CHOPPED

Wash the fenugreek leaves and set aside.

Cook the moong dhaal in lightly salted boiling water until it is soft. Drain and set aside.

Heat the oil in a heavy-based saucepan, add the onions, onions seeds and curry leaves and stir-fry until the onions are golden brown. Add the diced tomatoes and cook for 2 minutes. Lower the heat.

Next, add the ginger, garlic, chilli powder, ground fennel and salt and continue to stir-fry for a further 1 minute.

Stir in the fresh fenugreek leaves and continue to stir-fry, until the fenugreek is a shade darker.

Add the tinday and, if necessary, pour in the water. Cover the pan and cook until the tinday is soft and almost mushy.

Add the moong dhaal and green chillies. Cook for 1 more minute, transfer to a heated serving dish and serve while hot.

Stuffed Green and Red Peppers

(Bharay Huway Simla Mirch)

Peppers, like their close cousins, chillies, are now so common in Indian cooking that it's easy to forget that they were only introduced to the region in the 16th Century. They were probably first brought to Goa by the Portuguese, and spread through the rest of the country from there.

2 POTATOES

2 GREEN PEPPERS, HALVED AND DESEEDED

2 RED PEPPERS, HALVED AND DESEEDED

3 TABLESPOONS CORN OIL

½ TEASPOON ONION SEEDS

1 LARGE ONION, DICED

1 SMALL CAULIFLOWER, CUT INTO SMALL FLORETS

1 CARROT, DICED

50 G (2 OZ) SWEETCORN KERNELS

1 TEASPOON GINGER, SHREDDED

1½ TEASPOONS GROUND CORIANDER

1 TEASPOON GARLIC PULP

1 TEASPOON CHILLI POWDER

1 TABLESPOON TOMATO PURÉE

1 TABLESPOON LEMON JUICE

TO GARNISH

FRESH CORIANDER SPRIGS

CHOPPED GREEN CHILLIES

Cook the potatoes in boiling salted water. Once they are cooked, drain, then mash them down roughly and set aside. Put the prepared peppers in an ovenproof dish.

Heat the oil in a deep frying pan and fry the onion seeds for about 20 seconds. Add the onion and continue frying until golden brown. Next, add the cauliflower florets, diced carrots, sweetcorn and mashed potatoes, then add the ginger, ground coriander, garlic, chilli powder, tomato purée and lemon juice. Continue to stir-fry over a low heat for 3–5 minutes, cool the mixture slightly then use to stuff the peppers. Garnish with the fresh coriander and chopped green chillies.

Pour about 1 tablespoon of oil over the peppers to prevent them sticking and bake in a preheated moderate oven, 180°C (350°F), Gas Mark 4, for about 10–12 minutes.

LEFT: From top, Stuffed Green and Red Peppers (recipe above) and Marrow Koftas in a Creamy Sauce (recipe above, right).

Marrow Koftas in a Creamy Sauce

500–750G (1–1½ LB) MARROW

2 TABLESPOONS PLAIN FLOUR

2 TABLESPOONS GRAM FLOUR

1 TEASPOON CHILLI POWDER

1½ TEASPOONS GROUND CORIANDER

1 TEASPOON GARAM MASALA

1 TEASPOON SALT

¼ TEASPOON TURMERIC

1 TABLESPOON FRESH CORIANDER LEAVES

6 TABLESPOONS CORN OIL

CREAMY SAUCE

2 ONIONS, CHOPPED

2 TABLESPOONS TOMATO PURÉE

1 TEASPOON GARLIC PULP

1 TEASPOON GROUND CUMIN

1½ TEASPOONS GROUND CORIANDER

2 GREEN CHILLIES, CHOPPED

2 TEASPOONS COCONUT POWDER

1 TABLESPOON FRESH MINT

1 TABLESPOON FRESH CORIANDER

1 TEASPOON SALT

1 TABLESPOON NATURAL YOGURT

5 TABLESPOONS CORN OIL

2 TOMATOES, CUT INTO QUARTERS

125 ML (4 FL OZ) CREAM

Peel, deseed and roughly chop the marrow and boil until it is soft and mushy. Drain and squeeze out any excess moisture.

Mix the plain flour, gram flour, chilli powder, ground coriander, garam masala, salt, turmeric and fresh coriander together in a bowl and add to the marrow. Blend together and form the mixture into small balls, about the size of a golf ball.

Heat the oil in a karahi or deep frying pan and gently fry the koftas, moving them around in the oil so that they brown all over. Remove from the pan and set aside.

For the sauce, place the onions, tomato purée, garlic, ground cumin, ground coriander, green chillies, coconut powder, mint, fresh coriander, salt and yogurt in a food processor and blend together for about 1 minute, stopping once to stir the mixture with a spatula. Transfer to a bowl and set aside.

Heat the corn oil in a heavy-based saucepan until very hot and reduce the heat to medium before adding the onion and spice mixture. Cook, stirring occasionally to prevent it from catching at the bottom of the pan, for 5–7 minutes, lowering the heat, if necessary. Add the tomatoes, pour in the cream and stir to mix.

Gently drop the koftas into the sauce one by one. Partly cover the saucepan with a lid and cook over a low heat for about 3–5 minutes. Serve hot with rice.

Panir with Mushrooms in a Creamy Sauce

Mushrooms are not very widely used in India, but all Indian cooks enthusiastically adopt whatever interesting vegetables are to hand. It was in the north-west frontier state of Kashmir where mushrooms were most common in traditional cooking. Nowadays, they are often used by Indians living in other parts of the world. There are now a number of different kinds of mushrooms available, and I would use white, brown cap or chestnut mushrooms in this recipe. The rather subtle flavour of oyster mushrooms would, I think, be somewhat overwhelmed by the spices in this dish. Panir can be bought at specialist shops, or you can make your own from the recipe on page 67.

125 G (4 OZ) BUTTER

1 TABLESPOON CORN OIL

1 BAY LEAF

2 ONIONS, FINELY DICED

150 ML (¼ PINT) WATER

1 TEASPOON GARLIC PULP

1 TEASPOON GINGER PULP

1 TEASPOON GROUND CUMIN

1 TEASPOON GROUND CORIANDER

1 TEASPOON CHILLI POWDER

¼ TEASPOON TURMERIC

1 TABLESPOON SALT

75 G (3 OZ) BROCCOLI, CUT INTO TINY FLORETS

75 G (3 OZ) MUSHROOMS, SLICED

150 G (5 OZ) PANIR, CUT INTO CUBES

175 ML (6 FL OZ) SINGLE CREAM

1 TABLESPOON CHOPPED FRESH CORIANDER

2 RED CHILLIES, SLICED

Melt the butter with the corn oil in a heavy-based saucepan and fry the bay leaf and the onions until golden brown. Pour in the water, lower the heat, cover and cook for 3–5 minutes.

Meanwhile, mix together the garlic, ginger, ground cumin, ground coriander, chilli powder, turmeric and salt in a small bowl. Pour the mixture over the onions, which should now be cooked and fairly dry. Stir-fry for about 1 minute.

Add the broccoli, mushrooms and panir and blend together.

Stir in the cream, then the coriander and chillies. Cook for about 2 minutes, transfer to a serving dish and serve with rice.

Mushrooms in a Creamy Fennel Sauce

Fennel is not widely used in India as a vegetable. In fact, the Florence fennel variety, with its thick bulbous base, is not much grown there. The species used in India is grown for its seeds, which are a common ingredient in many spice mixtures. They have a distinctive aniseed taste, and just a single teaspoon of them in this recipe will give a delightfully fresh taste to the whole dish. Again, use ordinary white cultivated mushrooms, or the chestnut or brown cap mushrooms which I think seem to have a little more flavour than the common white variety.

75 G (3 OZ) BUTTER

1 TABLESPOON OIL

2 ONIONS, DICED

1 TEASPOON FENNEL SEEDS

1 BAY LEAF

1 TEASPOON GINGER PULP

1 TEASPOON GARLIC PULP

¼ TEASPOON TURMERIC, CRUSHED

1 TEASPOON BLACK PEPPERCORNS, CRUSHED

1 TEASPOON GROUND CORIANDER

3 GREEN CHILLIES, CHOPPED

250 G (8 OZ) MUSHROOMS

1 TEASPOON SALT

175 ML (6 FL OZ) SINGLE CREAM

2 TABLESPOONS CHOPPED FRESH CORIANDER

½ LARGE RED PEPPER, DESEEDED AND SLICED

Heat the butter and oil in a karahi or deep frying pan, over a medium heat. Add the onions, fennel seeds and the bay leaf and fry for 3–5 minutes.

Meanwhile, blend the ginger, garlic, turmeric, black pepper and ground coriander together in a small bowl. Stir the mixture into the onions and lower the heat.

Add the green chillies, mushrooms and salt and continue to stir-fry for a further 2 minutes.

Pour in the cream, then the fresh coriander, stirring the mixture with a wooden spoon.

Finally, add the sliced red pepper and serve.

Spicy Okra
(Masala Bhindi)

A delicious array of spices is used in this dish – their aroma will be enhanced by the first frying in hot oil. Turmeric, the spice that gives this dish its colour, is sometimes used instead of saffron, but it should be prized for its own qualities. When adding this spice, don't be tempted to increase the quantity in the belief that 'more is better' – it can be bitter if you use too much. The best turmeric is a good, deep orange, with a lovely musky taste. Be careful, because turmeric is a very powerful dye, and if you get it on your clothes it will be just about impossible to get out.

2 ONIONS, DICED

1 TEASPOON GINGER PULP

1 TEASPOON GARLIC PULP

¼ TEASPOON TURMERIC

1 TABLESPOON COCONUT POWDER

1 TABLESPOON SESAME SEEDS

1 TEASPOON SALT

1 TEASPOON GROUND CORIANDER

1 TEASPOON CHILLI POWDER

5 TABLESPOONS CORN OIL

½ TEASPOON MIXED FENUGREEK SEEDS, ONION SEEDS AND MUSTARD SEEDS

3 CURRY LEAVES

2 TABLESPOONS OIL

500 G (1 LB) OKRA, TRIMMED AND CUT INTO 2.5 CM (1 INCH) PIECES

2 RED CHILLIES, SLIT AND DESEEDED

Place the onions, ginger, garlic, turmeric, coconut powder, sesame seeds, salt, ground coriander and chilli powder in a food processor and blend to a pulp.

Heat 3 tablespoons of the oil in a medium-sized saucepan, add the seeds and curry leaves and fry for about 30 seconds. Stir in the onion and spice mixture and cook over a medium heat, stirring occasionally.

Heat the remaining oil in a deep frying pan, add the okra and lightly fry the pieces for about 2 minutes.

With a slotted spoon, remove the okra from the pan and add to the onions. Cook for a further 3–5 minutes before adding the red chillies. Serve with paratas (see page 103).

Fried Okra with Panir
(Thali Huwi Bhindi Aur Panir)

Okra is widely used in Caribbean and American Creole cooking, and also in Africa and Asia. You should be able to buy okra in supermarkets, as well as from specialist greengrocers and Asian supermarkets. When choosing it, make sure it is firm and fresh, with no soft spots. Check that the stalk end has not withered – a sure sign that it is past its best. Panir can also be bought at Asian supermarkets, or made at home, using the recipe on page 67.

6 TABLESPOONS CORN OIL

300 G (10 OZ) OKRA, TRIMMED AND CUT INTO 2.5 CM (1 INCH) PIECES

175 G (6 OZ) PANIR, CUT INTO CUBES

2 ONIONS, DICED

1 TEASPOON ONION SEEDS

4 CURRY LEAVES

1 TEASPOON SALT

1 TEASPOON CHILLI POWDER

1½ TEASPOONS GROUND CORIANDER

1 TEASPOON GINGER PULP

1 TEASPOON GARLIC PULP

2 TOMATOES, SLICED

1 TABLESPOON LEMON JUICE

1 TABLESPOON CHOPPED FRESH CORIANDER

Heat the oil in a karahi or deep frying pan, add the okra and fry until cooked – about 3–5 minutes. With a slotted spoon, remove the okra from the pan and drain on kitchen paper. Add the panir cubes to the pan and fry in the same way. With a slotted spoon, remove the panir from the pan and drain on kitchen paper.

Add the onions, onion seeds and curry leaves to the oil left in the pan and fry for about 5 minutes. Lower the heat and stir in the salt, chilli powder, ground coriander, ginger and garlic. Add the tomatoes, then return the okra and panir cubes to the pan, stirring gently to coat the vegetables in the spicy oil.

Sprinkle on the lemon juice and fresh coriander.

Heat through and transfer the okra and panir to a serving dish. Serve hot with rice or chapatis.

VARIATION
Fried Okra with Panir and Peas
A delicious addition to this recipe – cook about 125 g (4 oz) of frozen peas for 2–3 minutes, then add them to the other ingredients at the same time as the tomatoes.

Okra Stuffed with Coconut
(Bhindi Aur Narial)

This is a wonderful way to cook okra – which can be rather glutinous in some dishes. They are a very attractive shape, and take very well to simple stuffings. Try them also with the even spicier variation below. When preparing okra for this dish it is very important to dry them thoroughly after washing them, and before slitting them down the middle.

500 G (1 LB) OKRA
1½ TEASPOONS MANGO POWDER
3 TABLESPOONS DESICCATED COCONUT
1½ TEASPOONS GROUND CORIANDER
1 TEASPOON BROWN SUGAR
½ TEASPOON CRUSHED DRIED RED CHILLIES
1 TABLESPOON CHOPPED FRESH CORIANDER
4 TABLESPOONS CORN OIL
¼ TEASPOON ONION SEEDS
1 TABLESPOONS LEMON JUICE

Wash the okra and dry on absorbent kitchen paper. Slit each one down the middle, leaving the ends intact and set aside.

In a separate bowl, blend the mango powder, desiccated coconut, ground coriander, brown sugar, crushed red chillies and fresh coriander. Using a teaspoon, stuff each okra with as much of the spice mixture as possible.

Heat the oil in a frying pan with a lid, and fry the onion seeds. Lower the heat, lift the okra a few at a time and place them in the oil. When all the okra are in the frying pan, sprinkle any remaining spice mixture on top and pour the lemon juice over. Cover the pan and cook over a gentle heat for about 10–15 minutes, checking occasionally.

Serve with puris.

VARIATION
Okra Stuffed with Chillies and Sesame Seeds
Replace the stuffing ingredients above with 2 red or green fresh chillies, finely diced, mixed with 1 tablespoon sesame seeds. Stuff the okra, then proceed as in the main recipe.

RIGHT:*Below top, the deliciously spicy Okra Stuffed with Coconut (recipe above) and Stuffed Baby Aubergines (recipe above, right). Okra and aubergines are two well-travelled ingredients. Aubergines were native to India, but have found their way all over the world, and are especially popular in countries north, south and east of the Mediterranean. Okra probably originated in Africa or Asia, and is now well known as a major ingredient of the American Creole dish, Gumbo.*

Stuffed Baby Aubergines
(Bharay Huway Basun)

Aubergines are now available in many shapes, sizes and colours. My greengrocer has small round white ones (which justify their alternative name of 'eggplant'), larger, pear-shaped purple ones, and long, curved, purple striped ones. They are perfect for stuffing.

6 BABY AUBERGINES
4 TABLESPOONS SESAME SEEDS
6 TABLESPOONS CORN OIL
2 ONIONS, DICED
1½ TEASPOONS GROUND CUMIN
1½ TEASPOONS GROUND CORIANDER
1 TEASPOON CHILLI POWDER
1 TEASPOON SALT
1 TABLESPOON LEMON JUICE
1 TABLESPOON FRESH CORIANDER
2 POTATOES, PEELED AND ROUGHLY DICED
4 TOMATOES, ROUGHLY DICED
½ TEASPOON MIXED FENUGREEK SEEDS,
ONION SEEDS AND MUSTARD SEEDS
4–6 CURRY LEAVES
FRESH CORIANDER SPRIGS, TO GARNISH

Wash the aubergines and cut in half from the bottom end, leaving the stalk intact. Remove the soft flesh from the inside, leaving a thick shell. Set the aubergines aside.

Grind the sesame seeds to a rough texture.

Heat 3 tablespoons of the oil in a saucepan and fry the onions until golden brown. Add the ground cumin, coriander, chilli powder, salt, lemon juice, fresh coriander and potatoes and stir-fry for about 3 minutes over a medium heat.

Add the tomatoes and ground sesame seeds and continue to stir-fry for 3–5 minutes.

Lower the heat, cover the pan and continue cooking until the potatoes are tender. Remove the lid and continue cooking until the mixture is quite dry. Remove the pan from the heat and set aside to cool.

Stuff the aubergines with the cooled mixture.

Heat the remaining oil in a saucepan, add the whole mixed seeds and the curry leaves and fry for a few seconds. Lower the heat, add the aubergines gently one by one, cover the pan and continue cooking for about 15 minutes, or until the aubergines are soft but not mushy.

Serve, garnished with sprigs of fresh coriander.

Potatoes and Aubergines in Tamarind

(Aloo Baigun in Imli)

Tamarinds, known in India as 'imli', are the seed pods of a tree which grows all over South-east Asia, the Caribbean and tropical Africa. They are about the size of a garden pea pod, curved, with a lovely velvety brown coat. They have a sweet-and-sour flesh, which is used in many dishes, rather as you would use lemon juice in European cooking.

4 TABLESPOONS CORN OIL

½ TEASPOON MIXED ONION SEEDS,
MUSTARD SEEDS AND FENUGREEK SEEDS

2 ONIONS, SLICED

1 TEASPOON GINGER PULP

1½ TEASPOONS GROUND CORIANDER

1 TEASPOON GARLIC PULP

¼ TEASPOON TURMERIC

1 TEASPOON CHILLI POWDER

1 TABLESPOON TOMATO PURÉE

1 TABLESPOON TAMARIND PASTE

150 ML (¼ PINT) WATER

2 TABLESPOONS SUGAR

1 TEASPOON SALT

2 POTATOES, DICED

1 AUBERGINE, DICED

2 TOMATOES, QUARTERED

2 GREEN CHILLIES, CHOPPED

2 TABLESPOONS CHOPPED FRESH CORIANDER

Heat the oil in a heavy-based saucepan and add the onion seeds, mustard seeds and fenugreek seeds. Fry for about 20 seconds then add the onions, continuing to stir-fry until the onions are golden brown. Lower the heat and add the ginger, ground coriander, garlic, turmeric, chilli powder, tomato purée, tamarind paste, water, sugar and salt. Stir to mix.

Cover the saucepan and gently cook until the onions have softened and the sauce is thick.

Add the potatoes and aubergines, cover the pan again and cook, stirring occasionally, until the potatoes and aubergine are cooked. Stir in the tomatoes, green chillies and fresh coriander, transfer to a warmed serving dish and serve hot.

Aubergines and Potatoes

(Aloo Baigun)

These two vegetables go very well together. In European cooking, aubergines are usually salted first to remove the dark and bitter juices. However, boiling or steaming seems to remove those juices, and aubergines are delectable in this recipe.

5 TABLESPOONS CORN OIL

2 ONIONS, FINELY DICED

1 TABLESPOON TOMATO PURÉE

1½ TEASPOONS GROUND CORIANDER

1 TEASPOON GINGER PULP

1 TEASPOON GARLIC PULP

1½ TEASPOONS CHILLI POWDER

1 TEASPOON SALT

¼ TEASPOON TURMERIC

300 ML (½ PINT) WATER

2 POTATOES, DICED

1 AUBERGINE, DICED

2 TOMATOES, QUARTERED

2 TABLESPOONS LEMON JUICE

2 TABLESPOONS CHOPPED FRESH CORIANDER

Heat the oil in a heavy-based saucepan, add the onions and fry for about 5 minutes. While the onions are cooking, mix the tomato purée, ground coriander, ginger, garlic, chilli powder, salt and turmeric in a small bowl.

Once the onions are fried, pour the spice mixture into the saucepan, lowering the heat at the same time. Stir-fry for about 1 minute before stirring in the water. Cover the saucepan and cook over a low heat until the onions are soft and the sauce has thickened.

Add all the vegetables, cover the saucepan again and let the vegetables cook in the steam for about 5 minutes. Check the pan after 5 minutes or so, and if the the contents seem too dry add 150 ml (¼ pint) of water. Cook for a further 10 minutes.

Stir in the lemon juice and fresh coriander and serve hot with chapatis or rice.

Mooli Curry
(Mooli Ki Bhujia)

You may have tried mooli (also known as 'daikon' or Japanese radish) before in salads, such as the one on page 111 of this book. However, if you haven't cooked it before, this is a good recipe to try. In Indian shops, it is usually sold with its leaves attached, and both root and leaves may be used in the curry. If you prefer a milder curry, omit the ginger pulp and decrease the quantity of chillies.

500 G (1 LB) MOOLI, PEELED AND ROUGHLY CHOPPED

50 G (2 OZ) YELLOW MOONG DHAAL

600 ML (1 PINT) WATER

1 TABLESPOON CHOPPED FRESH CORIANDER

1 TEASPOON GARLIC PULP

3 TABLESPOONS CORN OIL

2 GARLIC CLOVES

1 X 2.5 CM (1 INCH) PIECE FRESH GINGER, SHREDDED

2 BUNCHES SPRING ONIONS, ROUGHLY CHOPPED

1 TEASPOON SALT

1 TEASPOON CRUSHED DRIED RED CHILLIES

2 GREEN CHILLIES, CHOPPED

Place the mooli, moong dhaal, water, fresh coriander, garlic and ginger pulp in a saucepan and bring to the boil. Cook until the mooli is soft enough to be squeezed by hand. Drain and squeeze out any excess water from the mooli and dhaal. Set aside.

Heat the oil in a heavy-based saucepan.

Add the garlic cloves and shredded ginger and fry for a few seconds, then add the spring onions, salt, crushed red chillies and green chillies.

Add the mooli and stir to mix, then continue to cook, stirring, over a low heat, for 3–5 minutes.

Serve the mooli curry hot with freshly made chapatis.

Fenugreek with Sesame Seeds
(Methi Ki Bhaaji Aur Thill)

A wonderful dish, using some of my favourite herbs and spices. If you find it difficult to buy fresh fenugreek, do try to grow it in your garden – it will repay the effort. When using fresh fenugreek always break the leaves off the stalks, as the flower and stalk can sometimes be bitter. Fenugreek's botanical name is 'Trigonella foenum-graecum', which means 'Greek hay'. The Romans used it widely, and imported it from Greece, hence its Latin name. The Egyptians, too, used it as a vegetable, and held it in such high regard that they used its seeds when embalming the Pharaohs. It is rarely used outside India nowadays, but the seeds form a very important ingredient in spice mixtures and also in European ready-made curry powders.

2 BUNCHES FENUGREEK LEAVES

5 TABLESPOONS CORN OIL

¼ TEASPOON ONION SEEDS

3 ONIONS, SLICED

2 TEASPOONS MANGO POWDER

1 TEASPOON GINGER PULP

1 TEASPOON GARLIC PULP

1 TEASPOON CHILLI POWDER

1 TEASPOON GROUND CORIANDER

150 ML (¼ PINT) WATER

2 TOMATOES, DICED

3 TABLESPOONS SESAME SEEDS

1 TABLESPOON CHOPPED FRESH CORIANDER

Break the fenugreek leaves from the stalks and wash them thoroughly. Drain and set aside.

Heat the oil in a heavy-based saucepan and fry the onion seeds and onions over a medium heat until they are soft and golden brown.

Lower the heat and add all the spices. Continue to stir-fry for about 2 minutes, then add the fenugreek leaves, and the water. Cover the pan and cook for 5–7 minutes.

Remove the lid from the saucepan and stir-fry until you begin to see some free oil on the sides of the pan.

Add the diced tomatoes, sesame seeds and chopped fresh coriander and gently mix together. Transfer to a warmed serving dish to serve.

Fresh Stir-fried Spinach with Coconut
(Thaazi Saag Aur Narial)

Saag, or spinach, is one of the most popular vegetables in Indian cooking. It is an all-purpose word for any number of leafy green vegetables, which vary according to the season and the region.

2 TABLESPOONS MASOOR DHAAL

750 G (1½ LB) FRESH SPINACH

2 ONIONS, ROUGHLY CHOPPED

1 RED CHILLI, CHOPPED

1 TEASPOON GINGER PULP

1 TEASPOON GARLIC PULP

1 TEASPOON SALT

1 TEASPOON CHILLI POWDER

2 TABLESPOONS LEMON JUICE

1 TEASPOON BROWN SUGAR

6 TABLESPOONS CORN OIL

1 TABLESPOON CHOPPED FRESH CORIANDER

2 TABLESPOONS DESICCATED COCONUT

Boil the masoor dhaal until soft, drain off all the water and then set aside.

Wash the spinach thoroughly, chop roughly and place in a saucepan with the water left on the leaves. Bring to the boil, drain thoroughly and set aside.

Place the onions, red chillies, ginger, garlic, salt, chilli powder, lemon juice and brown sugar in a food processor and grind for about 20–30 seconds until blended together.

Heat the oil in a saucepan, pour in the onion and spice mixture and stir-fry over a low heat for 3–5 minutes. Add the spinach, masoor dhaal, fresh coriander and half the desiccated coconut and continue to stir-fry for a further 3–5 minutes.

Transfer the spinach to a warmed serving dish, sprinkle over the remaining coconut and serve.

RIGHT: *Fresh Stir-fried Spinach with Coconut (recipe above) and Masala Vegetables (recipe above, right). Spinach is known as 'saag' in India – an all-purpose word which covers many green leafy vegetables. You could substitute similar ingredients, such as Swiss chard, beetroot tops or spring greens. The Masala Vegetable recipe could, similarly, be adapted to other vegetables in season.*

Masala Vegetables

'Masala' simply means a mixture of spices, and that mixture can vary according to its region of origin, the ingredients it is to accompany, and also the spices the cook has on the shelf at the moment. 'Garam masala' means 'hot spices', and is used in the cooking of North India. You will find it ready-made in most good food shops. There are mixtures that are used for other purposes, such as a tandoori masala, and other mixtures from the various regions of India. Garam masala contains cardamom seeds, nutmeg, cinnamon and mace – all spices popular in the cooler north. Southern masalas are fiery hot, and in Goa the mixtures often contain tamarind. You can buy it ready-made, or prepare it yourself by grinding the component spices.

2 TABLESPOONS COCONUT POWDER

2 TEASPOONS GROUND CORIANDER

1 TEASPOON CHILLI POWDER

½ TEASPOON CRUSHED BLACK PEPPERCORNS

1 TEASPOON GARAM MASALA

1 TEASPOON GARLIC PULP

1 TEASPOON GINGER PULP

¼ TEASPOON TURMERIC

1 TABLESPOON TAMARIND PASTE

1 TEASPOON SALT

1 TEASPOON POPPY SEEDS

150 ML (¼ PINT) WATER

5 TABLESPOONS CORN OIL

2 ONIONS, FINELY CHOPPED

1 SMALL CAULIFLOWER, BROKEN INTO SMALL FLORETS

1 LARGE CARROT, DICED

2 POTATOES, DICED

50 G (2 OZ) FROZEN PEAS

50 G (2 OZ) SWEETCORN KERNELS

1 TABLESPOON CHOPPED FRESH CORIANDER

2 RED CHILLIES

2 TEASPOONS SOFT BROWN SUGAR

In a bowl, mix the coconut powder together with the ground coriander, chilli powder, black pepper, garam masala, garlic, ginger, turmeric, tamarind, salt and poppy seeds. Stir in the water to form a paste.

Heat the oil in a heavy-based saucepan, add the onions and fry until golden brown. Pour the spice mixture into the onions and stir-fry over a low heat for 2–3 minutes.

Start to add the vegetables one by one, stirring all the time. Finally, add the fresh coriander, red chillies and brown sugar.

Cover the pan and steam cook the vegetables over a very low heat until they are all cooked. If the dish seems too dry to cook the vegetables by steaming, just add 150 ml (¼ pint) water to the pan. Serve with rice or chapatis.

Deep-fried Vegetables in Yogurt Sauce
(Thali Huwi Subzee Dhahee May)

Indian cooks don't use a great deal of oil when deep-frying, because they only cook a few items at a time. Here, each of the vegetables is deep-fried separately before being added to the yogurt mixture. The spices are then fried in another small pan before being sprinkled over the other ingredients.

475 G (15 OZ) NATURAL YOGURT
1 TABLESPOON FINELY CHOPPED FRESH MINT
1 TABLESPOON FINELY CHOPPED FRESH CORIANDER
1 TEASPOON SALT
1 TEASPOON SUGAR
2 GREEN CHILLIES, FINELY CHOPPED
150 ML (¼ PINT) WATER
300 ML (½ PINT) CORN OIL
2 POTATOES, DICED
125 G (4 OZ) GREEN BEANS
75 G (3 OZ) SWEETCORN KERNELS
1 CARROT, SLICED
½ CAULIFLOWER, CUT INTO FLORETS
2 TABLESPOONS CORN OIL
½ TEASPOON WHITE CUMIN SEEDS
½ TEASPOON ONION SEEDS
½ TEASPOON MUSTARD SEEDS
½ TEASPOON FENUGREEK SEEDS
6 CURRY LEAVES
½ TEASPOON GROUND CUMIN
½ TEASPOON GROUND CORIANDER
½ TEASPOON CHILLI POWDER
1 TABLESPOON CHOPPED FRESH CORIANDER

Whisk the yogurt in a large serving bowl and add the mint, coriander, salt, sugar, chillies and water. Whisk for a further minute and set aside.

Heat the oil in a karahi or deep frying pan to 190°C (375°F), or until a cube of bread browns in 30 seconds, add the potatoes and fry in batches until cooked. With a slotted spoon, remove from the pan with a slotted spoon and drain on absorbent kitchen paper. Repeat the frying process with all the vegetables. Add them to the yogurt mixture.

Heat the 2 tablespoons oil in a frying pan and fry all the seeds and the curry leaves for about 30 seconds. Pour the sizzling oil and seeds over the vegetables in yogurt.

Sprinkle the ground cumin, coriander and chilli powder over the yogurt and serve garnished with fresh coriander.

Stuffed Chillies
(Bhari Huwi Subzee)

Try to choose thick green and red chillies for this recipe, as they are easier to deseed and stuff than the thin chillies. Remember that the hottest parts of any chilli are the seeds and membranes, so be sure to remove them. Remember also not to touch your face, mouth or eyes with your fingers when you have been handling chillies – the juice is just as fiery as the vegetable itself.

175 G (6 OZ) PANIR
½ TEASPOON GARAM MASALA
½ TEASPOON SALT
1 TEASPOON MANGO POWDER
12 GREEN CHILLIES
12 RED CHILLIES
2 TABLESPOONS CORN OIL
1 TEASPOON MIXED ONION SEEDS, MUSTARD SEEDS, WHITE CUMIN SEEDS AND FENUGREEK SEEDS
1 TEASPOON CRUSHED DRIED RED CHILLIES
1 TABLESPOON LEMON JUICE

Cut the panir into thin strips to fit into the chillies.

Mix the garam masala, salt and mango powder together and pour the mixture on to the panir strips.

Cut both the red and green chillies in half horizontally, while keeping them intact at the top, and remove the seeds. Fill the chillies with the spicy panir.

Heat the oil in a karahi or deep frying pan, add all the seeds and crushed red chillies and fry for about 1 minute.

Gently drop in the stuffed chillies and fry them for about 2–3 minutes, moving them carefully in the pan to ensure that the filling does not fall out.

Transfer the stuffed chillies to a warmed serving dish and sprinkle the lemon juice on top. Serve while hot.

Cauliflower in a Hot and Sour Sauce

Another recipe using the lemony flavour of tamarind – the 'hot' provided by the spices, and the 'sour' by the tamarind.

175 G (6 OZ) RED TAMARIND PASTE

200 ML (½ PINT) HOT WATER

4–5 TABLESPOONS CORN OIL

1 TEASPOON MIXED ONION SEEDS,

MUSTARD SEEDS AND FENUGREEK SEEDS

5 CURRY LEAVES

2 ONIONS, DICED

½ TEASPOON TURMERIC

1 TEASPOON GROUND CUMIN

1½ TEASPOONS GROUND CORIANDER

1 TEASPOON GINGER PULP

½ TEASPOON GARLIC PULP

1 TEASPOON CHILLI POWDER

300 ML (½ PINT) WATER

1 TEASPOON SALT

1 CAULIFLOWER, CUT INTO FLORETS

4 RED CHILLIES, SLICED

2 TABLESPOONS CHOPPED FRESH CORIANDER

Break the tamarind paste down and soak it in the hot water for at least 15 minutes. Squeeze out the water and push the tamarind pulp through a sieve. Once all the pulp has been extracted, set aside in a bowl.

Meanwhile, heat the oil in a heavy-based saucepan, add the mixed seeds, curry leaves and onions and stir-fry for about 3 minutes. Add the turmeric, ground cumin, ground coriander, ginger, garlic, chilli powder, water and salt and cook for about 5–7 minutes. Add the tamarind pulp, cauliflower florets, red chillies and fresh coriander and mix all the ingredients well together. Cover and cook for 5–7 minutes.

Uncover the pan and stir-fry the cauliflower in its sauce for a further 2 minutes before serving.

Illustrated on page 33.

Cauliflower, Carrots and Potatoes in a Spicy Yogurt Sauce

(Masala Walay Dahee May Subzee)

This is a thoroughly spicy dish, perfect for adding interest to these rather mild vegetables.

½ CAULIFLOWER, BROKEN INTO SMALL FLORETS

2 POTATOES, DICED

2 CARROTS, SLICED

2 TEASPOONS SALT

300 ML (½ PINT) CORN OIL

475 G (15 OZ) NATURAL YOGURT

1 TEASPOON SUGAR

1 TABLESPOON CHOPPED FRESH MINT

2 GREEN CHILLIES, FINELY CHOPPED

1 TABLESPOON CHOPPED FRESH CORIANDER

1 TABLESPOON CORN OIL

¼ TEASPOON MUSTARD SEEDS

4 CURRY LEAVES.

Rub the vegetables with half the salt and set aside.

Heat the oil in a karahi or deep frying pan to 190°C (375°F), or until a cube of bread browns in 30 seconds, add the salted vegetables and fry them in the hot oil until cooked, but making sure they retain their texture and remain crunchy. Place the vegetables in a serving dish.

Blend the yogurt with the remaining salt, sugar, mint, green chillies and fresh coriander and pour over the vegetables.

Heat the tablespoon of oil in a frying pan, add the mustard seeds and curry leaves and fry for about 1 minute. Pour the seasoned oil over the yogurt and vegetables and serve.

VARIATIONS

Spicy Yogurt Sauce with Courgettes, Broccoli and Green Beans
A very colourful version of the main recipe – use yellow or green-and-white striped courgettes if available. Substitute 2–3 courgettes and 250 g (8 oz) green beans cut into 2.5 cm (1 inch) slices for the potatoes and carrots, and 2 large heads of broccoli, broken into florets, for the cauliflower. Proceed as in the main recipe.

Marrow and Pumpkin with Spicy Yogurt Sauce
Another colourful variation, especially if you can find the best variety of pumpkin – small, with dense, quite dry, very brilliant orange flesh and dark green skin. Substitute about 250–300 g (8–10 oz) peeled, deseeded and diced marrow and 250–300 g (8–10 oz) peeled, deseeded and diced pumpkin instead of the potatoes, carrots and cauliflower. Proceed as in the main recipe.

Courgettes and Carrots in Olive Oil

(Sarson Kay Thail May Subzee)

Olive oil, that staple of Mediterranean cooking, is not widely used in India as a cooking medium. It is more common as a beauty aid – combed through hair to make it healthy and glossy, or as a massage oil for babies. Interestingly enough, mustard oil, typically used in Bengali cuisine, is also used as a massage oil for babies. Unlike mustard itself, the oil is rich and mild. However – Indian cooks love to adopt fine ingredients such as olive oil, and this recipe is a perfect example. It is important not to overcook the courgettes, otherwise they will lose their shape and their delicate flavour.

2 LARGE COURGETTES, SLICED
2 LARGE CARROTS, SLICED
2 TABLESPOONS OLIVE OIL
2 BUNCHES SPRING ONIONS, CHOPPED
4 GARLIC CLOVES, HALVED
6–8 MINT LEAVES
1 TABLESPOON CHOPPED FRESH CORIANDER
1 TABLESPOON LEMON JUICE
2 TABLESPOONS MALT VINEGAR
1 TABLESPOON SUGAR
1 TABLESPOON SALT
1 GREEN CHILLI, FINELY CHOPPED

Blanch the courgettes and carrots in boiling water for about 3–5 minutes. Drain and set aside.

Heat the olive oil in a karahi or deep frying pan and fry the spring onions and garlic cloves together for about 2 minutes. Stir in the courgettes and carrots, then the mint, coriander, lemon juice, malt vinegar, sugar, salt and green chilli.

Gently stir-fry until the vegetables are cooked, making sure the vegetables retain their shape.

Transfer to a serving dish and serve immediately.

Spicy Fried Peas and Sweetcorn

(Masala Matar Aur Bhutta)

This makes a very good side dish and is also very popular with children. Serve it together with a pulao or biryani, with a dhaal, some pickles and bread or poppadums.

10 BABY POTATOES, THICKLY SLICED
3 TABLESPOONS CORN OIL
1 ONION, DICED
300 G (10 OZ) FROZEN SWEETCORN KERNELS
250 G (8 OZ) FROZEN PEAS
1 TEASPOON SALT
1 TEASPOON CHILLI POWDER
1 TABLESPOON CHOPPED FRESH CORIANDER
1 TABLESPOON LEMON JUICE
1 RED PEPPER, DESEEDED AND DICED
2 TOMATOES, SLICED

Blanch the baby potatoes for about 5 minutes in lightly salted boiling water, drain and set aside.

Heat the oil in a karahi or deep frying pan, add the diced onion and stir-fry until golden brown.

Lower the heat and add the sweetcorn, peas, salt and chilli powder and cook for 5–7 minutes, stirring occasionally to prevent it from catching at the bottom. Mix in the freshly chopped coriander and the lemon juice, then add the potatoes and red pepper and cook for a further 5–7 minutes. Serve, garnished with the sliced tomatoes.

VARIATION
Spicy Fried Peppers and Carrots
Another delicious and colourful recipe to serve with this sauce. Substitute 300 g (10 oz) red or yellow peppers, deseeded and finely diced, in place of the sweetcorn, and 250 g (8 oz) diced carrot instead of the peas. Proceed as in the main recipe.

RIGHT: *Spicy Fried Peas and Sweetcorn (recipe above, right) and Courgettes and Carrots in Olive Oil (recipe above). Courgettes are a variety of marrow or squash, so you could substitute either of those vegetables if preferred – or the attractive, pale green, pear-shaped chayotes, also known as 'chow-chows' or 'chokos'.*

Vegetables in a Creamy Saffron Sauce
(Zafrani Subzee)

An ideal dish for a special dinner party. The vegetables are cooked in a rich aromatic sauce and should be served with Pea Pulao (recipe on page 97). Saffron is a very elegant ingredient, in both taste and appearance, and its presence in a dish usually indicates a Moghul or Persian ancestry.

450 ML (¾ PINT) FRESH SINGLE CREAM
1 TABLESPOON TOMATO PURÉE
1½ TEASPOONS GARAM MASALA
1 TEASPOON GINGER PULP
1 TEASPOON GARLIC PULP
1 TEASPOON CHILLI POWDER
2 TABLESPOONS GROUND ALMONDS
¼ TEASPOON GROUND CINNAMON
¼ TEASPOON GROUND CARDAMOM
1 TEASPOON SALT
300 ML (½ PINT) WATER
½ TEASPOON SAFFRON STRANDS, CRUSHED
75 G (3 OZ) BUTTER
1 TABLESPOON OIL
1 ONION, DICED
¼ TEASPOON BLACK CUMIN SEEDS
3 COURGETTES, SLICED
3 CARROTS, SLICED
½ CAULIFLOWER, CUT INTO SMALL FLORETS
125 G (4 OZ) PEAS
1 TABLESPOON CHOPPED FRESH CORIANDER, TO GARNISH

Mix the cream, tomato purée, garam masala, ginger, garlic, chilli powder, almonds, cinnamon, cardamom, salt, water and saffron strands together in a bowl and set aside.

Melt the butter with the oil in a medium-sized saucepan over a medium heat. Add the diced onion and black cumin seeds and fry for 3–5 minutes.

Add all the vegetables and stir-fry for a further 3 minutes before pouring in the sauce and stirring well to mix.

Lower the heat, cover and cook for 7–10 minutes.

Garnish the vegetables with fresh coriander before serving.

Potato and Carrot Stir-fry
(Thalay Huway Aloo Aur Gajar)

A quick and easy last-minute recipe, perfect for family meals, or as an extra dish when you suddenly find you have an unexpected guest.

4 TABLESPOONS CORN OIL
4 CURRY LEAVES
1 TEASPOON FENNEL SEEDS
½ TEASPOON WHITE CUMIN SEEDS
1 TEASPOON CRUSHED DRIED RED CHILLIES
2 ONIONS, SLICED
1 TEASPOON GINGER PULP
1 TEASPOON GARLIC PULP
¼ TEASPOON TURMERIC
12 BABY POTATOES, CUT INTO
5 MM (¼ INCH) THICK SLICES
2 CARROTS
1 GREEN PEPPER, DESEEDED AND DICED
2 TABLESPOONS LEMON JUICE
2 RED CHILLIES, SLICED

Heat the oil in a heavy-based saucepan, add the curry leaves, fennel seeds, cumin seeds and dried red chillies and fry for about 30 seconds.

Add the sliced onions and continue to stir-fry until some of the onion slices are darker than others. Lower the heat and gradually add the ginger, garlic and turmeric.

Add the vegetables, stirring continuously. Lower the heat to very low, cover the pan and steam-cook for 7–10 minutes.

When the vegetables are cooked, sprinkle on the lemon juice and serve, garnished with the sliced red chillies.

Hot and Spicy Cauliflower
(Mirch Masala Gobi)

A very spicy recipe from Northern India.

2 ONIONS, SLICED

1 TEASPOON GARAM MASALA

1 TEASPOON GROUND CUMIN

1½ TEASPOONS GROUND CORIANDER

2 GREEN CHILLIES

1 TEASPOON GINGER PULP

1 TEASPOON SALT

¼ TEASPOON TURMERIC

1 TABLESPOON TOMATO PURÉE

2 TABLESPOONS LEMON JUICE

3 TABLESPOONS OIL

½ TEASPOON WHITE CUMIN SEEDS

½ TEASPOON CORIANDER SEEDS, CRUSHED

4 DRIED RED CHILLIES

4 CURRY LEAVES

1 CAULIFLOWER, CUT INTO SMALL FLORETS

Place the sliced onions, garam masala, ground cumin, ground coriander, green chillies, ginger, salt, turmeric, tomato purée and lemon juice in a food processor, grind for about 1 minute and then set aside.

Heat the oil in a heavy-based saucepan, add the cumin seeds, coriander seeds, dried red chillies and curry leaves and fry for about 30 seconds. Then add the onion and spice mixture to the pan and stir-fry for about 5 minutes.

Finally, add the cauliflower florets, cover the pan and cook over a low heat for 7–10 minutes, checking occasionally to prevent the mixture sticking to the bottom of the pan.

Serve the cauliflower hot with rice, and a dhaal from the Pulses chapter on pages 76–89.

Spicy Stir-fried Cauliflower
(Thali Huwi Masala Gobi)

Cauliflower is a very good stir-fried vegetable. It cooks quickly, holds its shape, and its mild flavour is well enhanced by spices and aromatics. A favourite with Indian cooks.

50 G (2 OZ) CHANA DHAAL

½ TEASPOON MIXED FENNEL SEEDS,
CORIANDER SEEDS, WHITE CUMIN SEEDS

4 WHOLE DRIED RED CHILLIES

4 GARLIC CLOVES, SLICED

1 X 3.5 CM (1½ INCH) PIECE FRESH GINGER, SHREDDED

4 TABLESPOONS CORN OIL

1 BUNCH SPRING ONIONS, CHOPPED

½ GREEN PEPPER, DESEEDED AND SLICED

½ CAULIFLOWER, CUT INTO FLORETS

1 TEASPOON SALT

1 TEASPOON CHILLI POWDER

2 TOMATOES, CUT INTO QUARTERS

2 TABLESPOONS CHOPPED FRESH CORIANDER

Pick over the chana dhaal (small yellow split peas) for any stones or other foreign bodies, then wash and drain them. Boil until soft but not mushy, drain, then set aside.

Mix the seeds, chillies, garlic and ginger together in a small bowl and set aside.

Heat the oil in karahi or deep frying pan, lower the heat, add the whole spice mixture and fry for about 1 minute. Add the spring onions and fry for 2–3 minutes, then add the green pepper, cauliflower, salt and chilli powder, and continue to stir-fry gently for a further 5–7 minutes.

Finally, add the chana dhaal, tomato quarters and fresh coriander. Blend the mixture together and transfer to a serving dish. Serve with Masala Puri (recipe on page 102).

VARIATION
Spicy Stir-fried Green Vegetables
Other vegetables may be substituted for the cauliflower, such as broccoli, broken into florets, peas, runner beans, cut into 2.5 cm (1 inch) slices, and topped and tailed mangetout. Mangetout are not a typical Indian vegetable, but they lend themselves very well to this spicy stir-fry.

Other pulses, such as black-eye beans, may be substituted for the yellow chana dhaal.

Vegetables in a Pasanda-style Sauce
(Subzee Kay Pasanday)

Pasanda sauces, typified by the use of yogurt, ground almonds and spices, are traditionally used in non-vegetarian dishes. However, when used with vegetables they are, if anything, even more delicious. They have their origins in Northern India, but are now so popular they are eaten all over the country, including in the vegetarian south. Some people like to dry-roast the spices before cooking, but these days spices are of such high quality that they are often used just as they are.

250 G (8 OZ) NATURAL YOGURT
3 TABLESPOONS GROUND ALMONDS
2 TEASPOONS POPPY SEEDS
1 TEASPOON GARLIC PULP
1 TEASPOON GINGER PULP
¼ TEASPOON TURMERIC
1½ TEASPOONS CHILLI POWDER
1 TEASPOON GARAM MASALA
4 GREEN CARDAMOM PODS
½ TEASPOON BLACK CUMIN SEEDS
4 TABLESPOONS CORN OIL
2 ONIONS, DICED
250 G (8 OZ) CANNED TOMATOES WITH THEIR JUICE
1 LARGE POTATO, DICED
1 CARROT, SLICED
1 BABY CAULIFLOWER, CUT INTO SMALL FLORETS
3 RED CHILLIES, SLIT DIAGONALLY
2 TABLESPOONS CHOPPED FRESH CORIANDER
150 ML (¼ PINT) WATER

Whisk the yogurt with a fork or a whisk and set aside.

In a saucepan dry roast the ground almonds and poppy seeds, shaking the pan continuously, for about 1 minute. Remove from the heat and pour on to the yogurt. Then add the garlic, ginger, turmeric, chilli powder, garam masala, the cardamoms and black cumin seeds.

Heat the oil in a heavy-based saucepan, add the onions and fry until golden brown. Stir in the yogurt and spice mixture, lower the heat and fry for 1–2 minutes. Pour in the tomatoes, stirring continuously. Add the vegetables, then the red chillies and fresh coriander.

Stir in the measured water, lower the heat further, cover the pan and cook for 5–7 minutes, or until the vegetables are cooked through.

Serve the vegetables hot with a rice dish.

Green Chillies in Sesame Seeds
(Hari Mirch Aur Thill)

Try to choose the small but thick green chillies for this recipe as they are easier to deseed. When slitting them, leave them intact at the top. Sesame's botanical name is 'Sesamum indicum', which betrays its Indian origin. It is now widely used all over the world, but nowhere more widely than in India and China.

175 G (6 OZ) SESAME SEEDS
4 TABLESPOONS CORN OIL
15 GREEN CHILLIES, SLIT LENGTHWAYS AND DESEEDED
¼ TEASPOON WHITE CUMIN SEEDS
3 DRIED RED CHILLIES
4 CURRY LEAVES
1½ TEASPOONS GROUND CORIANDER
1 TEASPOON GINGER PULP
1 TEASPOON GARLIC PULP
1 TEASPOON CHILLI POWDER
2 TABLESPOONS LEMON JUICE
1 TABLESPOON CHOPPED FRESH CORIANDER
150 ML (¼ PINT) WATER

Dry roast the sesame seeds (see page 8) and grind them in a food processor or a spice grinder until they are powdery.

Heat the oil in a karahi or deep frying pan, add the green chillies and fry them for about a minute. Using a slotted spoon, remove from the oil and set aside.

Lower the heat and sprinkle the cumin seeds, dried red chillies and curry leaves into the pan. Fry for 10 seconds. Remove the pan from the heat and add the ground sesame seeds, then the ground coriander, ginger, garlic, chilli powder, lemon juice and fresh coriander.

Return the pan to a very low heat and stir-fry, adding the water, for about 5 minutes. Finally, add the fried green chillies and serve hot.

LEFT: *From top, Green Chillies in Sesame Seeds (recipe above) and Vegetables in a Pasanda-style Sauce (recipe above, left).*

Stuffed Tomatoes
(Aloo Bharay Tamatar)

Long-grain rice is used in this recipe rather than Basmati. Try to use a good quality long-grain rice as it is a delicious recipe.

75 G (3 OZ) BUTTER

1 TABLESPOON OIL

1 ONION, DICED

½ TEASPOON BLACK CUMIN SEEDS

1 TEASPOON GINGER PULP

1 TEASPOON GARLIC PULP

1 TEASPOON CHILLI POWDER

1 TABLESPOON TOMATO PURÉE

1 TABLESPOON GROUND CORIANDER

1 CUP LONG-GRAIN RICE

50 G (2 OZ) SWEETCORN KERNELS

50 G (2 OZ) GREEN PEPPER, DICED

50 G (2 OZ) FROZEN PEAS

1 CARROT

1 TEASPOON SALT

3 TABLESPOONS LEMON JUICE

1 TABLESPOON CHOPPED FRESH CORIANDER

2 CUPS WATER

6–8 LARGE AND FIRM TOMATOES

TO GARNISH

2 POTATOES, THINLY SLICED

1 TEASPOON SALT

1 TEASPOON CRUSHED RED CHILLIES

OIL FOR DEEP-FRYING

2 FRESH CHILLIES

2 TOMATOES, SLICED

Heat the butter and oil in heavy-based saucepan, add the onion and cumin seeds and fry until golden brown. Lower the heat, and stir in the remaining ingredients except the whole tomatoes and the garnish. Bring to the boil, lower the heat, cover the saucepan tightly and cook for 10–15 minutes.

Meanwhile, cut the tops off the tomatoes, scrape out the flesh and seeds and set the shells and tops aside.

When cooked, cool the rice mixture slightly and spoon it into the tomatoes. Put the tops on the tomatoes, place in an ovenproof dish and cook in a preheated moderate oven, 180°C (350°F), Gas Mark 4 for 10–15 minutes.

Prepare the garnish; rub the potato slices with the salt and crushed red chillies. Heat the oil in a karahi or deep frying pan to 180°C (350°F), or until a cube of bread browns in 30 seconds. Add the potato slices in batches and deep-fry until they are golden. Remove with a slotted spoon and drain on kitchen paper. Place the fried potato slices around the cooked tomatoes and garnish with the chillies and tomato slices.

Panir-stuffed Tomatoes
(Panir-Bharay Tamatar)

These tomatoes are filled with a spicy bean mixture, which, with the panir, makes them very nutritious. You could also serve them as a starter. You can buy the panir from specialist shops, or make your own from the recipe on the opposite page.

50 G (2 OZ) BLACK-EYE BEANS

8–10 FIRM TOMATOES

4 TABLESPOONS CORN OIL

1 ONION, FINELY DICED

1 TEASPOON GROUND CORIANDER

1 TEASPOON GINGER PULP

1 TEASPOON CHILLI POWDER

1 TEASPOON SALT

1 TEASPOON CHOPPED FRESH CORIANDER

75 G (3 OZ) PANIR, CHOPPED INTO SMALL DICE

(SEE RECIPE, RIGHT)

1 TEASPOON LEMON JUICE

Boil the black-eye beans in lightly salted water until soft but not mushy. Drain and set aside.

Meanwhile, carefully cut the tops off the tomatoes and set aside. Remove the flesh from the tomatoes and put the tomato shells in an ovenproof dish.

Heat the corn oil and fry the onions until golden brown. Lower the heat and add all the spices, including the salt, and the black-eye beans and blend together.

Add the fresh coriander, panir and lemon juice. Stir-fry for 2–3 minutes and leave to cool.

Spoon the cooled mixture into the tomatoes. Cover with the tomato tops and bake in a preheated moderate oven, 180°C (350°F), Gas Mark 4, for 15–20 minutes. Serve the tomatoes with chapatis or rice.

VARIATION

Panir-stuffed Courgettes or Acorn Squash

This recipe may be adapted to other vegetables, such as courgettes or acorn squash. Both these vegetables may need to cook a little longer in the oven than tomatoes. Test after 15 minutes, and cook longer, if required. Acorn squash is a variety of pumpkin, which is delicious with nutmeg, so you could also add ½ teaspoon ground nutmeg.

Stir-Fried Baby Onions with Panir

This makes an attractive dish for a dinner party. As it is a fairly dry dish, I suggest you choose any curry or dhaal which has a sauce to serve with it. You can buy panir from Asian delicatessens, or make your own, using the recipe on this page.

1 TABLESPOON CORN OIL

75 G (3 OZ) BUTTER

1½ TEASPOONS GARAM MASALA

1 TEASPOON GARLIC PULP

1 TEASPOON GINGER PULP

1 TEASPOON SALT

1 TEASPOON CHILLI POWDER

1 TABLESPOON TOMATO PURÉE

15 BABY ONIONS, PEELED AND LEFT WHOLE

250 G (8 OZ) PANIR, CUT INTO 2.5 CM (1 INCH) CUBES (SEE RECIPE, RIGHT)

175 G (6 OZ) SWEETCORN KERNELS

125 G (4 OZ) PEAS

6 GREEN CHILLIES

2 TABLESPOONS CHOPPED FRESH CORIANDER

10–12 CHERRY TOMATOES

1 LIME, SLICED

Heat the corn oil and butter in a heavy-based saucepan. Turn the heat off so that the oil is cooled a little. While the oil is cooling, mix all the spices with the tomato purée and pour the mixture into the oil and butter. Turn the heat up to medium, add the whole onions and panir cubes and fry for 3 minutes, stirring continuously.

Gradually add the sweetcorn and peas. Continuing to stir-fry, add the whole green chillies, freshly chopped coriander and whole cherry tomatoes. Cover the pan and cook for about 3 minutes before serving, garnished with the lime slices.

Illustrated on page 32.

Panir

Panir, also known as 'paneer' is not a dish in itself – rather, it is an ingredient in many Indian dishes, vegetarian or otherwise. You will find it extensively used in recipes throughout this book. This is an ingredient which is very, very important in Indian cooking, especially vegetarian. Together with pulses, it is a major source of protein. It has been called 'Indian cottage cheese', but I don't think this does it justice at all. Cottage cheese or ricotta could be used in some recipes (at a pinch), but the real thing is available in Asian supermarkets, and is not too much trouble to make yourself. Just allow enough time when you first try this recipe, and it will soon become second nature.

1 LITRE (1¾ PINTS) FULL CREAM MILK, OR HALF CREAM AND HALF FULL CREAM MILK

3 TABLESPOONS LEMON JUICE

Pour the milk into a saucepan, and bring to the boil. Remove from the heat and stir in the lemon juice. Bring back to the boil and keep stirring until the milk curdles.

Line a sieve with muslin, and pour in the curdled milk. Bring the edges of the muslin together and gently squeeze out the whey, or liquid part of the curdled milk. What is left is a rather crumbly kind of cheese, called 'chenna panir'. You can use it in some salads and other dishes in this form, but I prefer it in its next stage, true panir. To achieve this, wrap the chenna in muslin, and shape into a rectangular block. Place a wooden board on top, and a weight (such as a tin of beans) on top of the board. After about 2 hours, the cheese will have firmed up and become panir.

Cut the panir into cubes and use as described in the recipes, which include:

Panir and Vegetable Samosas on page 30,

Vegetable Jalfrezi on page 36,

Vegetables in a Rich Creamy Sauce on page 38,

Shahi Panir Koftas on page 39,

Methi and Spinach Panir on page 47,

Panir with Mushrooms in a Creamy Sauce on page 50,

Fried Okra with Panir on page 51,

Stuffed Chillies on page 58,

Panir-stuffed Tomatoes on page 66 and

Stir-fried Baby Onions with Panir on page 67.

NOTE

An alternative, and perhaps easier way of making panir is to keep the chenna wrapped in muslin, put it back in the sieve, place a plate and weight on top and leave for 2 hours. The shape would not be as tidy as the rectangular block, but it is as easy to use as mozzarella.

Stuffed Green Chillies on Fried Onions
(Pyaaz Bhari Hari Mirch)

Try to choose the large thick variety of green chillies for this recipe. Not only are they easier to stuff, but they are sometimes not as hot as the thinner variety.

4 TABLESPOONS SESAME SEEDS

2 TEASPOONS GROUND CORIANDER

3 TEASPOONS MANGO POWDER

1 TEASPOON SALT

1 TEASPOON CHILLI POWDER

2 TABLESPOONS LEMON JUICE

1 TEASPOON SOFT SUGAR

1 TABLESPOON WATER

10–12 GREEN CHILLIES

4 TABLESPOONS CORN OIL

½ TEASPOON ONION SEEDS

3 ONIONS, DICED

TO GARNISH

FRESH CORIANDER

LEMON WEDGES

Dry roast the sesame seeds, shaking the saucepan all the time to prevent them from burning. Roast the seeds until some bits are darker than others. Remove the pan from the heat and transfer to a dish to cool.

Meanwhile, mix the ground coriander, mango powder, salt, chilli powder, lemon juice, sugar and water together in a bowl.

Once the sesame seeds have cooled, put in a food processor or a spice grinder and grind until they are powdery. Blend them with the spice mixture; if you find that it is too dry, stir in a little water to make a very thick paste.

Prepare the green chillies by slitting them in the middle, making sure they remain intact at the ends.

Fill the split chillies with the spice mixture.

Heat the oil in a karahi or deep frying pan, carefully add the stuffed chillies, about 4 at a time, and fry until they are cooked. Remove from the oil and set aside.

Fry the onion seeds and onions in the oil remaining in the pan over a medium heat for 5–7 minutes, then transfer to a serving dish. Place the fried chillies on top of the onions and serve garnished with lemon wedges and fresh coriander.

Bitter Gourds with Onions
(Karela Aur Pyaaz)

Bitter gourds, called karela in India, are probably the least-known Asian vegetable in the West. You will recognize them by their prickly green skins. It is important to soak them in salted water to draw out some of the very bitter taste.

2 BITTER GOURDS

2 TEASPOONS SALT

4 TABLESPOONS OIL

½ TEASPOON MUSTARD SEEDS

3 ONIONS, SLICED

1 TEASPOON GARLIC PULP

1½ TEASPOONS GROUND CORIANDER

1 TEASPOON GINGER PULP

¼ TEASPOON TURMERIC

1 TEASPOON CHILLI POWDER

1 TEASPOON POPPY SEEDS

2 TABLESPOONS LEMON JUICE

2 FRESH RED CHILLIES, SLICED

1 TABLESPOON CHOPPED FRESH CORIANDER

Wash, peel and slice the bitter gourds. Rub the salt into the slices and set aside for about 2 hours.

Wash the bitter gourds under cold running water, rubbing them with your fingers to remove some of the seeds. Wash at least twice and set aside.

Heat the oil in a heavy-based saucepan, add the mustard seeds and sliced onions and fry over a medium heat for about 4 minutes. Lower the heat and add the garlic, the ground coriander, ginger, turmeric, chilli powder and poppy seeds. Stir well. Add the bitter gourd slices, then the lemon juice, red chillies and freshly chopped coriander.

Continue to cook, stirring, for a further 3 minutes.

Cover the saucepan with a lid and cook for another 2 minutes before serving the bitter gourds with chapatis.

VARIATION
Cucumbers with Onions
If you are unable to buy bitter gourds in your greengrocers (though they are widely available now, even in supermarkets), this recipe is also delicious made with cucumbers. They should also be salted for 10–15 minutes before cooking, not because they are bitter, but because the salt will draw out some of the moisture in the vegetable so it will be firmer when cooked. Substitute 2 small or 1 large cucumber for the 2 bitter gourds, and proceed as in the main recipe.

RIGHT: *Illustrated here, from the top, are Stuffed Green Chillies on Fried Onions (recipe above) and Bitter Gourds (also known as Karela) with Onions (recipe above, right).*

Panir and Vegetable Roghan Josh
(Panir Aur Subzee Ka Roghan Josh)

You will love this tomato-based curry with its elegant, creamy sauce. Traditionally made with lamb, this dish has successfully been made vegetarian by using panir instead.

3 TABLESPOONS CORN OIL
250 G (8 OZ) PANIR, CUBED (SEE PAGE 67)
150 G (5 OZ) NATURAL YOGURT
50 G (2 OZ) GROUND ALMONDS
1½ TEASPOONS GARAM MASALA
1 TEASPOON GARLIC PULP
1 TEASPOON GINGER PULP
1 TEASPOON CHILLI POWDER
1½ TEASPOONS SALT
A PINCH OF TURMERIC
6 TABLESPOONS OIL
1 X 2.5 CM (1 INCH) PIECE CINNAMON STICK
4 WHOLE BLACK PEPPERCORNS
4 WHOLE GREEN CARDAMOMS
1 BAY LEAF
1 LARGE ONION, SLICED
1 X 425 G (14 OZ) CAN TOMATOES
2 TABLESPOONS LEMON JUICE
1 LARGE CARROT, SLICED
2 COURGETTES, SLICED
1 GREEN PEPPER, DESEEDED AND ROUGHLY DICED
150 ML (¼ PINT) WATER
2 TABLESPOONS CHOPPED FRESH CORIANDER
2 GREEN CHILLIES, CHOPPED
FLAKED ALMONDS, TO GARNISH

Heat the oil in a karahi or deep frying pan, add the panir cubes and fry until it has some colour, making it lightly crisp and golden on the outside. Remove with a slotted spoon and drain on absorbent kitchen paper.

Whisk the yogurt, add the almonds, garam masala, garlic, ginger, chilli powder, salt and turmeric. Set aside.

In a medium-sized saucepan, heat the oil over a medium heat, add the whole spices and fry for about 30 seconds, then add the onion and fry until golden brown.

Pour the yogurt and spice mixture into the pan and stir-fry. Add the tomatoes and their juice and the lemon juice, followed by the carrot, courgettes and green pepper and continue to stir-fry over a medium heat for a further 2 minutes. Pour in the water, cover the pan and cook over a low heat for 3–5 minutes.

Uncover, stir in the coriander, chillies and panir, spoon into a serving dish and garnish with flaked almonds.

Illustrated on page 123.

Potatoes and Leeks in a Creamy Sauce

Leeks are not very widely used in Indian cooking, but they are perhaps the mildest of the onion family. They originated in the Middle East, and are more closely identified with European cooking than Indian. However, this dish is not particularly spicy, so the rather delicate flavour of leeks can be more easily appreciated.

600 ML (1 PINT) WATER
10–12 BABY POTATOES, THICKLY SLICED
2 LEEKS, CLEANED AND SLICED
75 G (3 OZ) BUTTER
1 TABLESPOON CORN OIL
½ TEASPOON FENNEL SEEDS
1 BAY LEAF
½ TEASPOON CORIANDER SEEDS, CRUSHED
½ TEASPOON BLACK PEPPERCORNS, CRUSHED
1 TEASPOON SALT
175 ML (6 OZ) SINGLE CREAM
1 TABLESPOON CHOPPED FRESH CORIANDER

Bring the water to the boil, add the potatoes and leeks and blanch for about 5 minutes. Remove the pan from the heat, drain and set aside.

Heat the butter and oil in a heavy-based saucepan over a medium heat, add the fennel seeds, the bay leaf, crushed coriander seeds and black peppercorns and fry for 15 seconds.

Gradually add the potatoes and leeks and stir gently, being careful not to break the potato slices. Add the salt, cream and freshly chopped coriander, cover the pan and cook for about 5 minutes more.

Check that the potatoes are cooked before transferring to a serving dish. This dish is good served as an accompaniment.

Potatoes with Peas
(Aloo Matar)

This is probably among the more popular vegetarian curries – there is hardly one which is better-known – and it is found on almost every Indian or Pakistani restaurant menu.

2 TABLESPOONS TOMATO PURÉE

1 TEASPOON GROUND CORIANDER

1 TEASPOON CHILLI POWDER

1 TEASPOON GARAM MASALA

1 TEASPOON GARLIC PULP

½ TEASPOON TURMERIC

1 TEASPOON SALT

1 TABLESPOON LEMON JUICE

3 TABLESPOONS CORN OIL

2 ONIONS, DICED

125 G (4 OZ) PEAS

300 ML (½ PINT) CORN OIL

3 POTATOES, ROUGHLY DICED

2 TABLESPOONS CHOPPED FRESH CORIANDER

½ GREEN PEPPER, DESEEDED AND SLICED

½ RED PEPPER, DESEEDED AND SLICED

Mix the tomato purée, ground coriander, chilli powder, garam masala, garlic, turmeric, salt and lemon juice together in a bowl and set aside.

Heat the oil in a frying pan, add the onions and fry until golden brown. Pour the tomato purée and spice mixture into the pan, lower the heat and stir-fry for about 3 minutes. Stir in the peas and set aside.

Heat the remaining corn oil in a karahi or deep frying pan to 180°C (350°F), or until a cube of bread browns in 30 seconds, add the potatoes and fry them until they have golden edges and are cooked through. Remove the potatoes dice from the pan and add to the peas and spice mixture.

Finally, add the fresh coriander and sliced green and red peppers and stir-fry for a further 2 minutes. Serve the dish hot.

Stir-fry Cabbage with Green Mango
(Thali Huwi Bund Gobi Aur Kairi)

The mangoes used in this stir-fry are green or unripe ones. They are used in cooked dishes in preference to the ripe ones because they have a sweet-and-sour taste. When mangoes first arrive at the greengrocers, they are very often green, sometimes needing many days to ripen. They can be used in the green, hard state, or you can buy special green mangoes in Asian and Caribbean greengrocers. There are hundreds of varieties of mango in India – and people have quite heated debates about which one is the best for this purpose or that.

Be careful when peeling mangoes – they have a white, sticky sap, especially in the stalk, and it can burn your skin a little if you don't wash your hands immediately after peeling the fruit.

2 GREEN MANGOES

½ SMALL WHITE CABBAGE, GRATED FINELY

2 CARROTS, COARSELY GRATED

2 ONIONS, SLICED

1 LARGE RED PEPPER, DESEEDED AND SLICED

5 TABLESPOONS CORN OIL

1 TEASPOON MUSTARD SEEDS

4 WHOLE CURRY LEAVES

1 X 3.5 CM (1½ INCH) PIECE FRESH GINGER, SHREDDED

3 GREEN CHILLIES, SLICED LENGTHWAYS

150 ML (¼ PINT) WATER

1 TABLESPOON CHOPPED FRESH CORIANDER

Peel each mango, take out and discard the stone, and cut into two. Dice roughly and put in a bowl with the cabbage, carrots, onions and red pepper.

Heat the oil in a heavy-based saucepan, add the mustard seeds, curry leaves and shredded ginger and fry over a medium heat until they are a shade darker.

Stir in the green mangoes and vegetables and stir-fry for about 5 minutes. Add the green chillies and then, the water. Cover the pan and cook for 5–7 minutes.

Remove the lid, mix in the fresh coriander, and serve hot, with chapatis, if liked.

Illustrated on page 123.

Aloo Saag

One of the best-known of all Indian vegetable dishes in the West. Aloo Saag – literally Potatoes and Spinach – is a winning combination in many different cuisines, but probably never better than in this dish.

4 TABLESPOONS CORN OIL

1 ONION, CHOPPED

4 CURRY LEAVES

6–8 FENUGREEK SEEDS

¼ TEASPOON ONION SEEDS

2 TOMATOES, SLICED

1 TEASPOON GARLIC PULP

1 TEASPOON CHILLI POWDER

1½ TEASPOONS GROUND CORIANDER

1 TEASPOON SALT

1½ TEASPOONS MANGO POWDER

6–8 NEW POTATOES

250 G (8 OZ) FROZEN SPINACH

150 ML (¼ PINT) WATER

2 RED CHILLIES, SLICED

2 TABLESPOONS CHOPPED FRESH CORIANDER

10–12 PIECES SHREDDED GINGER, TO GARNISH (OPTIONAL)

Heat the oil in a heavy-based saucepan and fry the onion, curry leaves, fenugreek and onion seeds until they have changed colour. Lower the heat to medium and add the tomatoes, garlic, chilli powder, ground coriander, salt and mango powder.

Stir-fry for 3–5 minutes before adding the potatoes and spinach. Continue to stir-fry for a further 5 minutes.

Pour in the water, cover the pan and cook over a low heat for 10–15 minutes. When the potatoes are cooked through, add the red chillies and fresh coriander. Mix thoroughly and transfer to a serving dish. Garnish with the shredded ginger pieces, if liked. This dish is best served with chapatis.

Stir-fried Mushrooms
(Thalay Huway Kumbi)

Though mushrooms are not very widely used in India, they are much appreciated by Indians living in other parts of the world. Use ordinary white, cultivated mushrooms, or varieties such as chestnut or brown cap. You could also substitute button mushrooms, which would give this dish a very attractive appearance – they will go a pretty yellow, thanks to the turmeric in the spices.

3 TABLESPOONS CORN OIL

2 ONIONS, SLICED

1 TEASPOON FENNEL SEEDS

125 G (4 OZ) PEAS

1 TEASPOON GARLIC PULP

¼ TEASPOON TURMERIC

2 GREEN CHILLIES

1 TEASPOON CHILLI POWDER

1 TEASPOON SALT

2 TABLESPOONS CHOPPED FRESH CORIANDER

500 G (1 LB) MUSHROOMS, THICKLY SLICED

Heat the oil in a deep frying pan and fry the onions and the fennel seeds for about 3 minutes, or until soft. Add the peas, garlic, turmeric, green chillies, chilli powder and salt and stir-fry over a medium heat for another 3 minutes. Add the freshly chopped coriander and mushrooms and continue to fry for about 5 minutes, stirring gently, until the onions are cooked through.

Transfer the mushrooms to a serving dish and serve hot with puris or baby poppadums.

VARIATION
Stir-fried Mangetout with Baby Corn
A delicious and colourful variation. Substitute 500 g (1 lb) baby corn and 125 g (4 oz) mangetout for the mushrooms and peas. Add the baby corn at the same time as the fresh coriander, and the mangetout about 1 minute before serving.

LEFT: *From the top, Aloo Saag (recipe above, left) and Stir-fried Mushrooms (recipe above). Mushrooms are not widely used in India, other than in Kashmir, in the far north-west. This dish is also delicious made with mangetout and baby corn.*

Vegetable Balti

Balti dishes have become very popular recently – the Indian dish of the moment. Their fame in Britain seems to have started in Birmingham, and from there balti houses seem to have sprung up in every large city. These dishes originate in Pakistan and in the area the British Raj knew as the wild North-west Frontier. They are named after the pan in which they are cooked – a double-handled, wok-like metal pot. Everyone seems to be buying balti pans nowadays, but you can also use an ordinary karahi, a wok or even deep frying pan. In restaurants, balti dishes are cooked and served in the same pan.

125 G (4 OZ) BLACK-EYE BEANS

8 BABY POTATOES

1 LARGE CARROT, THICKLY SLICED

1 HEAD OF BROCCOLI, CUT INTO 8 SMALL FLORETS

6 TABLESPOONS CORN OIL

1 ONION, SLICED

½ TEASPOON ONION SEEDS

4 CURRY LEAVES

3 CLOVES GARLIC

2 TOMATOES, SLICED

1 TEASPOON CHILLI POWDER

1 TEASPOON SALT

4 GREEN CHILLIES, THICKLY SLICED

1 TABLESPOON CHOPPED FRESH CORIANDER

Cook the black-eye beans in simmering water until soft.

Cook the potatoes and carrots in boiling salted water, then cut the potatoes in half. Set aside.

Heat the oil in a karahi or wok, add the onion, onion seeds and curry leaves, followed by the garlic.

Stir-fry for about 2 minutes, then add the tomatoes, chilli powder and salt. Stir-fry for a further 30 seconds.

Add the potatoes, carrots and broccoli florets, then the black-eye beans. Continue to stir-fry for a further 3–5 minutes. Add the green chillies and fresh coriander, cover with foil and simmer for a further 2 minutes. Serve with accompaniments such as rice, naan or other Indian breads, dhaal and other vegetable dishes.

Balti Vegetables in a Spicy Sauce with Panir

An interesting variation on the basic vegetable balti. Panir, that special, easy-to-make-yourself Indian cheese, is wonderful for cooking. It holds its shape and doesn't melt into strings the way ordinary cheese does. It can be bought at Asian supermarkets, or made at home using the recipe on page 67. Feel free to experiment with balti dishes – many of the other stir-fried curries in this chapter can be happily adapted to the balti method of cooking.

4 TABLESPOONS CORN OIL

½ TEASPOON MUSTARD SEEDS

3 TABLESPOONS TOMATO PURÉE

175 ML (6 FL OZ) WATER

1 TEASPOON GRATED FRESH ROOT GINGER

½ TEASPOON CRUSHED FRESH GARLIC

1 TEASPOON GROUND CORIANDER

1 TEASPOON GARAM MASALA

1 TEASPOON SALT

½ TEASPOON BROWN SUGAR

175 G (6 OZ) FROZEN PEAS

6-8 SMALL FLORETS OF CAULIFLOWER

1 COURGETTE, SLICED

1 CARROT, DICED

2 RED CHILLIES, SLICED

1 TABLESPOON CHOPPED FRESH CORIANDER

8–10 CUBES OF PANIR (SEE PAGE 67)

125 ML (4 FL OZ) SINGLE CREAM

Heat the corn oil in a karahi or wok, add the mustard seeds and cook for about 30 seconds. Lower the heat.

Whisk the tomato purée with the water. Add the ginger, garlic, ground coriander, garam masala, salt and brown sugar. Pour into the karahai or wok, and stir continuously for about 2 minutes.

Add the vegetables, one by one, stirring to mix. Add the chillies, fresh coriander and panir and cook for a further 3 minutes. Pour in the cream, stir to blend, then serve.

Thali

Thalis are the most common vegetarian meals in India. Although native to South India, they are now found all over the sub-continent. You will find them in most restaurants, from the local version of a 'three-star' to the simplest village 'caff', where the usual metal tray may be supplanted by a banana leaf! You will even be served thalis when travelling by train, especially in the south – and very good they are too. Your order is taken at one station and telegraphed ahead to the next one. The thali is then freshly prepared and delivered to your seat at the next station. Briefly, a thali is usually served on a round metal tray with high sides, rather like a wide, shallow cake tin. In the centre is a mound of rice, which is surrounded by 'katoris' – small dishes of various curries, dhaals, chutneys, curd (yogurt) and other accompaniments. You flavour the rice with some or all of these dishes, according to taste or appetite.

If you were ordering this dish in a restaurant, your plate would be constantly replenished until you had, literally, eaten all you could. Paan can be served at the end of any Indian meal, to freshen the palate after its adventures with so many different spices. They are often available in Asian delicatessens. If you are unable to find them, they may be omitted, or a small dish of dried fennel seeds substituted. Thalis are traditionally eaten with the fingers in India, but a spoon or fork does equally well if your 'finger-food' skills are not very highly developed!

2 CUPS BASMATI RICE

3 CUPS WATER

½ TEASPOON SALT

KATORIS

A SELECTION OF KATORIS, FOR EXAMPLE:

RASAM (PAGE 82)

SAMBHAR (PAGE 84)

RAITA (PAGE 108)

CHUTNEYS OR PICKLES (PAGES 106–7)

CURRIES (PAGES 34–72)

CURD

1 PINT GREEK YOGURT, OR HOME-MADE YOGURT, MADE WITH

600 ML (1 PINT) FULL CREAM MILK AND

2 TABLESPOONS NATURAL YOGURT

OTHER ACCOMPANIMENTS

DHAAL

POPPADUMS

PURIS OR DOSAI (OPTIONAL)

FRESH RADISHES, FRESH CHILLIES,

LEMON WEDGES, SLICED TOMATOES

OR ONIONS (OPTIONAL)

PAAN, FENNEL SEEDS OR NUTS (OPTIONAL)

Rice

To prepare the rice, first wash it in various changes of water until the water runs clear. This removes the starches which would otherwise make the rice grains stick together. Cook in a rice-cooker, following the manufacturer's instructions.

Alternatively, wash the rice as described above, then place in a pan with water to the proportion of 2 cups of rice to 3 cups of water, and ½ teaspoon of salt. Bring to the boil, then cover and reduce the heat to the lowest temperature and simmer for about 25 minutes. Remove from the heat and rest, covered for about 10 minutes more.

Katoris

Serve a selection of vegetable curries, pickles and chutneys, which could include those listed in the ingredients, or others from this book.

Curd

If using ready-prepared yogurt, spoon into small dishes and place on the thali. To prepare your own, bring the milk to the boil in a large pan, stirring constantly.

Remove from the heat and set aside to cool for 10 minutes. Skim any skin from the surface. Whisk 2 tablespoons of yogurt in a small bowl, then stir into the warm milk. Whisk further until the mixture is slightly frothy. Cover the bowl with a clean tea towel and set aside in a warm place for 8 hours or overnight for the yogurt to thicken. Place in the refrigerator until ready to serve.

Dhaal

Choose a dish from the Pulses chapter on pages 76–89.

Poppadums, Puris or Dosai

No thali would be complete without the popular crunchy breads, poppadums, available in a variety of spicy flavours from supermarkets. If liked, puris (recipes on page 102) or dosai (recipe on page 22) may also be included.

Fresh vegetables

Fresh salad vegetables such as radishes, tomato or lemon wedges, sliced onions or spring onions, give a fresh, sharp contrast to the katoris. A few fresh chillies are often included.

Paan, Fennel Seeds or Nuts

Paan can be bought from Indian delicatessens in many flavour combinations. They are not an essential part of a thali and are something of an acquired taste.

To serve

Place a quantity of rice on the side of each tray. Working clockwise from the rice, place small dishes of katoris and dhaal around each thali tray, followed by poppadums, chutneys or pickles, and (if using), fresh vegetables, paan, fennel seeds or nuts. Diners add the other dishes to the rice, one by one according to taste. Serve extra rice separately.

Pulses

The pulses which are staples of Indian cooking –
lentils, split peas and dried beans – are high in
protein, an essential element in well-balanced
vegetarian cooking. In this chapter you will find
recipes for using all these pulses in many different
dishes. Remember that pulses, especially beans, are
best combined in a meal with a grain, such as rice
or bread, and perhaps a dairy product.

Masoor Dhaal with Vegetables
(Masoor Ki Dhaal Aur Subzee)

Masoor dhaal is the common split red lentil found in supermarkets all over the world.

125 G (4 OZ) MASOOR DHAAL
6 TABLESPOONS CORN OIL
¼ TEASPOON ONION SEEDS
6 WHOLE CURRY LEAVES
2 ONIONS, SLICED
1½ TEASPOONS GROUND CORIANDER
1 TEASPOON GINGER PULP
1 TEASPOON GARLIC PULP
1 TEASPOON CHILLI POWDER
1½ TEASPOONS SALT
3 GREEN CHILLIES
1 POTATO, ROUGHLY DICED
2 TABLESPOONS CHOPPED FRESH CORIANDER
3 TOMATOES, SLICED
2–3 TABLESPOONS LEMON JUICE

Wash the masoor dhaal thoroughly before boiling it in unsalted water until soft but not mushy. Drain and set aside.

In a karahi or a deep frying pan (with a lid) heat the oil and sprinkle in the onion seeds and curry leaves. After 10 seconds, add the onions and fry until golden brown.

Lower the heat and add all the spices and salt.

Next, chop 2 of the green chillies, and add to the pan with the potatoes. Stir-fry for about 3 minutes before adding the dhaal, then the fresh coriander, tomatoes and the remaining green chilli, chopped. Blend the mixture together, then pour in the lemon juice, cover the pan and cook for 5–7 minutes.

Lentils with a Butter Dressing
(Tarica Dhaal)

Another recipe using masoor dhaal, this time with a butter dressing. Butter has a particular significance in India, where the cow is a sacred animal, and butter and ghee are used in religious ceremonies. Ghee, or clarified butter, is available in Asian grocers and some supermarkets. As described on page 46, you can also make your own by melting ordinary unsalted butter over a low heat. Simmer for about 45 minutes until the white milk solids separate out. Strain the clear golden ghee through muslin before using.

175 G (6 OZ) MASOOR DHAAL
600 ML (1 PINT) WATER
1 TEASPOON GINGER PULP
½ TEASPOON GARLIC PULP
1 TEASPOON GROUND CORIANDER
1 TEASPOON SALT
½ TEASPOON TURMERIC
FOR THE BAGHAAR TARICA
1 TABLESPOON CORN OIL
75 G (3 OZ) BUTTER
½ TEASPOON ONION SEEDS
3 WHOLE GARLIC CLOVES
1 ONION, SLICED
2 TOMATOES, SLICED
1 GREEN CHILLI, CHOPPED
1 TABLESPOON CHOPPED FRESH CORIANDER, TO GARNISH

Wash the lentils. Place in a heavy-based saucepan, pour in the water, cover and bring to the boil. Add the ginger, garlic, ground coriander, salt and turmeric. Cover the saucepan again and cook slowly for 5 minutes. Remove the pan from the heat.

Using a wooden masher, mash the lentils. The dhaal should now have a consistency similar to thick soup. Spoon into a serving dish.

For the baghaar tarica, heat the oil and the butter in a frying pan over a medium heat, add the onion seeds, garlic, onion, tomato and green chilli and fry for about 2 minutes. Remove the pan from the heat and pour over the dhaal.

Serve garnished with the freshly chopped coriander.

PREVIOUS PAGES: *From left, Green Mango Dhaal (Kairi Ki Dhaal) (recipe page 79), and Bitter Gourds with Chana Dhaal (Karela Dhaal) (recipe page 84). Green or unripe Indian mangoes (known as 'ambi' or 'kairi', available from around February to June or July, are used to give curries and various lentils a sweet/sour flavour. Bitter gourds should be salted before use, to draw out the bitter juices.*

Green Mango Dhaal
(Kairi Ki Dhaal)

There are hundreds of different varieties of mango in India. They are used ripe, to be eaten fresh or used in cooking, especially in chutneys. There is also a special variety of very juicy, sweet mango known rather bluntly as 'sucking mangoes'. You squeeze and knead the fruit until it's quite soft, then cut a small hole in one end and suck out the sweet juice – a good way of avoiding the fibrous strings you find in some varieties. Mangoes are also used green or unripe, when they are known as 'ambi' or 'kairi'. These are available from about February to June or July and are used to give curries and various lentils a sweet/sour flavour. Mangoes often arrive in the shops unripe, so you should be able to find them in greengrocers or supermarkets quite easily.

2 GREEN MANGOES

175 G (6 OZ) MASOOR DHAAL

5 TABLESPOONS CORN OIL

2 BUNCHES SPRING ONIONS, CHOPPED INTO 4 CM (1½ INCH) PIECES

4 GREEN CHILLIES, CHOPPED

½ TEASPOON WHITE CUMIN SEEDS

½ TEASPOON GINGER PULP

½ TEASPOON GARLIC PULP

1 TEASPOON CHILLI POWDER

1 TEASPOON GROUND CORIANDER

2 TABLESPOONS CHOPPED FRESH CORIANDER

Wash, peel and roughly slice the mangoes, discarding the stone in the middle. Put the mango slices in a bowl, cover and set aside.

Wash and inspect the lentils for any stones etc. Boil the lentils in plenty of lightly salted water until soft but not mushy, drain and set aside.

Meanwhile, heat the oil in a heavy-based saucepan, add the spring onions, mango slices, green chillies, cumin seeds, ginger and garlic and stir-fry, coating in the oil. Lower the heat and add the chilli powder and ground coriander. Stir-fry for about 3–5 minutes. Pour in the cooked lentils and continue to stir-fry gently, being careful not to mash the dhaal, for about 1 minute.

Finally, add the fresh coriander, cover the pan and cook for about 5 minutes over a very low heat.

Serve the Green Mango Dhaal hot.

Illustrated on page 76.

Whole Masoor Dhaal Khitchri

Khitchri, from Tamil Nadu in South India, is the 'grandfather' of that famous dish of the British Raj, kedgeree. This version is made with whole masoor, which is not as common as the split salmon-coloured lentils, but it is delicious and has a very good texture. As in other recipes in this chapter, use the same cup to measure the rice, lentils and water.

2 CUPS BASMATI RICE

1 CUP WHOLE MASOOR DHAAL

3 TABLESPOONS GHEE

2 ONIONS, SLICED

¼ TEASPOON ONION SEEDS

¼ TEASPOON MUSTARD SEEDS

6 CURRY LEAVES

¼ TEASPOON TURMERIC

1 TEASPOON GINGER PULP

1 TEASPOON GARLIC PULP

1½ TEASPOONS SALT

6 DRIED RED CHILLIES

2 POTATOES, DICED

3 GREEN CHILLIES

4 CUPS WATER

Wash the rice and lentils together, drain them into a sieve and then set aside.

Melt the ghee in a medium-sized saucepan, add the onions, onion seeds, mustard seeds and curry leaves and fry for 2 minutes. Lower the heat and add the remaining spices.

Next, add the potatoes and green chillies and stir-fry for about 2 minutes before mixing in the rice and lentils. Using a slotted spoon, continue to stir-fry gently for another minute.

Pour in the water, bring to the boil, lower the heat, cover the pan, and cook for 15–20 minutes, or until the rice is tender and all the water has been absorbed.

Pasta with Mangetout and Red Kidney Beans

Red kidney beans are sweet-tasting and the beans most often used in Mexican cooking. They are available dried or canned. Preparing them in their dried form can be a little complicated, so I find it much simpler and easier to use the canned variety.

50 G (2 OZ) PASTA SHELLS
2 ONIONS, ROUGHLY DICED
2 TABLESPOONS TOMATO SAUCE
1 TEASPOON CHILLI POWDER
1 TEASPOON GARLIC PULP
¼ TEASPOON TURMERIC
1½ TEASPOONS SALT
2 TABLESPOONS LEMON JUICE
1 TEASPOON SUGAR
125 G (4 OZ) BUTTER
1 TABLESPOON CORN OIL
½ TEASPOON ONION SEEDS
125 G (4 OZ) MANGETOUT, BLANCHED
50 G (2 OZ) CANNED RED KIDNEY BEANS, DRAINED
1 TABLESPOON FRESH CORIANDER
2 RED CHILLIES, SLICED

Cook the pasta in boiling salted water until it is tender. Drain and set aside.

Place the diced onions, tomato sauce, chilli powder, garlic, turmeric, salt, lemon juice and sugar in a food processor or blender. Blend for about 1 minute or until a soft, smooth paste is formed.

Melt the butter with the oil and onion seeds in a deep frying pan, add the spice mixture and fry for about 5–7 minutes, stirring continuously. Add the pasta, then the mangetout, red kidney beans, fresh coriander and red chillies and mix gently until well coated with the spice mixture.

Serve immediately with an Indian bread.

LEFT: From top, Baby Cauliflower with Toor Dhaal (recipe above, right) and Pasta with Mangetout and Red Kidney Beans (recipe above). Many supermarkets now stock baby vegetables such as cauliflowers, which make a very elegant dish. Though mangetout is not a traditional Indian vegetable, its fresh taste and texture are perfectly complemented by the spice mixture.

Baby Cauliflower with Toor Dhaal

This makes a very good dinner party dish, especially as good-quality baby vegetables are now readily available in supermarkets and greengrocers for much of the year.

3–4 BABY CAULIFLOWERS
2 TABLESPOONS TOOR DHAAL
300 ML (½ PINT) WATER
4 TABLESPOONS OIL
4 CURRY LEAVES
¼ TEASPOON MUSTARD SEEDS
¼ TEASPOON FENUGREEK SEEDS
1 TEASPOON GARLIC PULP
1½ TEASPOONS CHILLI POWDER
1 TEASPOON GINGER PULP
1½ TEASPOONS GROUND CORIANDER
¼ TEASPOON GROUND FENUGREEK
1 TEASPOON SALT
2 TABLESPOONS LEMON JUICE
3 RED CHILLIES, CHOPPED
2 TABLESPOONS CHOPPED FRESH CORIANDER
1 X 425 G (14 OZ) CAN TOMATOES
TO GARNISH
3 TOMATOES, QUARTERED
2 LIMES, SLICED

Cook the baby cauliflowers whole in lightly salted boiling water until tender but still intact. Drain the cauliflowers and set aside in a serving dish.

Wash and pick over the lentils for any stones etc, then cook them in the measured water until soft but not mushy. Drain and then set aside.

Heat the oil in a karahi or deep frying pan, add the curry leaves, mustard seeds and fenugreek seeds and fry gently for about 30 seconds.

Mix the garlic, chilli powder, ginger, ground coriander, ground fenugreek, salt, lemon juice, red chillies, fresh coriander and the tomatoes with their juice in a bowl. Pour the mixture into the seasoned oil and stir-fry for 5–7 minutes over a low heat. Add the lentils and cook for 2 minutes more.

Pour the mixture over the top of the cauliflower, garnish with the tomato quarters and lime slices and serve.

Toor Dhaal with Tomatoes
(Tomatar Dhaal)

Toor dhaal, also known as 'toovar dhaal', is a yellow split lentil, and there is also a pink variety. It has an interesting, dark, earthy flavour and is used in all the regions of India. You will sometimes find it coated in castor oil as a preservative, but this will be washed off when you boil it.

175 G (6 OZ) TOOR DHAAL

300 ML (½ PINT) WATER

SALT

4 TABLESPOONS CORN OIL

1 TEASPOON MUSTARD SEEDS

1 x 425 G (14 OZ) CAN TOMATOES

1 TEASPOON GINGER PULP

1 TEASPOON CHILLI POWDER

1 TEASPOON GARLIC PULP

1 TEASPOON GROUND CUMIN

1½ TEASPOONS GROUND CORIANDER

¼ TEASPOON GROUND FENUGREEK

¼ TEASPOON GROUND FENNEL

1½ TEASPOONS SALT

2 TABLESPOONS LEMON JUICE

50 G (2 OZ) BUTTER

1 SMALL ONION, CHOPPED

2 GREEN CHILLIES, CHOPPED

Wash the lentils and then boil in the lightly salted water until soft. When cooked, mash down to a paste, using a wooden masher. If necessary, add about 300 ml (½ pint) water to lighten the consistency.

Heat the oil in a heavy-based saucepan and gently fry the mustard seeds.

Mix the canned tomatoes with their juice, the ginger, chilli powder, garlic, ground cumin, ground coriander, fenugreek, fennel, salt and lemon juice in a small bowl and add to the pan with the mustard seeds.

Stir-fry the mixture for 2 minutes, pour in the lentils and lower the heat to medium. Cook, partly covered, for 1 minute.

Meanwhile, melt the butter in a frying pan over a medium heat, add the chopped onion and green chillies and fry for about 3 minutes.

Transfer the lentils to a warmed serving dish and pour the fried onion and chillies, with the butter in which they were fried, over the lentils. Serve immediately.

Rasam

'Rasam' is the Tamil word for 'essence', and this one is an essence of lentils, in this case toor dhaal. Eaten widely in South India, the basic rasam is flavoured and seasoned with a variety of spices and other ingredients, which can include ginger, mustard seeds, chillies, peppercorns, cumin, asafoetida, curry leaves and, often, the cooling edge of tamarind.

125 G (4 OZ) RED TAMARIND BLOCK

150 ML (¼ PINT) HOT WATER

175 G (6 OZ) TOOR DHAAL

750 ML (1¼ PINTS) WATER

1 TEASPOON SALT

¼ TEASPOON TURMERIC

1 TEASPOON GROUND CUMIN

1½ TEASPOONS GROUND CORIANDER

¼ TEASPOON BLACK PEPPERCORNS, CRUSHED

½ TEASPOON CRUSHED DRIED RED CHILLIES,

1 TEASPOON GARLIC PULP

2 TOMATOES, QUARTERED

2 TABLESPOONS CORN OIL

½ TEASPOON WHITE CUMIN SEEDS

6 CURRY LEAVES

3 FRESH GREEN CHILLIES

Break down the tamarind block. Pour the hot water over the tamarind and leave it to soak for about 10-15 minutes. Squeeze out all the water and push the tamarind through a sieve to extract the pulp.

Wash the lentils, put in a saucepan with the measured water, bring to the boil and cook over a medium heat. When the lentils are soft, add the salt, turmeric, ground cumin, ground coriander, crushed black peppercorns, chillies and garlic and then mash the dhaal down with a wooden masher.

Add the tomato quarters and the tamarind pulp and cook for about 2 minutes.

Meanwhile, heat the corn oil in a saucepan, add the cumin seeds, curry leaves and green chillies and fry for 1 minute. Pour the mixture over the dhaal, and serve hot.

Toor Dhaal with Spring Onions

Spring onions are best used fresh or very quickly stir-fried, as in Chinese or Vietnamese cooking. This is the way they are used in this colourful dish – a lively counterpoint to the tomatoes, green pepper and green chillies.

125 G (4 OZ) LENTILS (TOOR DHAAL)
450 ML (¾ PINT) WATER
4 TABLESPOONS OIL
¼ TEASPOON WHITE CUMIN SEEDS
4 GARLIC CLOVES, SLICED
1 X 5 CM (2 INCH) PIECE FRESH GINGER, SHREDDED
4 DRIED RED CHILLIES
1 LARGE BUNCH SPRING ONIONS, CHOPPED
2 TOMATOES, CHOPPED
1 GREEN PEPPER, DESEEDED AND SLICED
2 GREEN CHILLIES, FINELY CHOPPED
2 TABLESPOONS LEMON JUICE
1 TEASPOON SALT
1 TABLESPOON CHOPPED FRESH CORIANDER

Boil the lentils in the measured water until they are soft but not mushy and set aside.

Meanwhile, heat the oil in a medium-sized saucepan, add the whole cumin seeds and fry for 10 seconds, then lower the heat and add the garlic, ginger, dried red chillies, spring onions, tomatoes, green pepper and green chillies and stir-fry for about 3 minutes.

Pour the lentils over the mixture and continue to stir-fry for a further 2 minutes before adding the lemon juice, salt and the chopped fresh coriander.

Serve the toor dhaal hot with chapatis.

VARIATIONS

This recipe can also be made in a number of different ways. Instead of the toor dhaal, you could substitute a similar quantity of chickpeas, black-eye beans, red kidney beans, or a mixture of all three to produce a very colourful dish. You could also substitute ordinary diced onions or finely sliced leeks for the chopped spring onions.

Lentil and Vegetable Patties

These patties can either be served as a snack any time of the day or as part of a vegetarian meal. If you decide to serve them as a snack, serve with one of the chutneys from this book.

1 TABLESPOON TOOR DHAAL
2 POTATOES, DICED
2 CARROTS, DICED
1 ONION, DICED
½ CAULIFLOWER, CUT INTO SMALL FLORETS
2 GREEN CHILLIES, CHOPPED
1 TABLESPOON CHOPPED FRESH CORIANDER
2 TABLESPOONS CORN OIL
¼ TEASPOON ONION SEEDS
1 TEASPOON GINGER PULP
1 TEASPOON GARAM MASALA
1 TEASPOON CHILLI POWDER
1½ TEASPOONS SALT
1 TABLESPOON LEMON JUICE
OIL FOR SHALLOW-FRYING

Wash the lentils and boil in lightly salted water until soft but not mushy. Remove from the heat and set aside (still in the cooking water) while preparing the rest of the ingredients.

Put the potatoes, carrots, onion, cauliflower, green chillies and fresh coriander into a saucepan with water to cover and cook until the vegetables are soft. Drain and set aside.

Heat the oil in a karahi or a deep frying pan, add the onion seeds and fry until they turn a shade darker. Add the cooked vegetables, the drained lentils, ginger, garam masala, chilli powder, salt and lemon juice. Stir so that all the ingredients are combined well together.

Transfer the mixture into a large bowl and leave to cool.

Using a fork, break off small balls from the mixture, about the size of a golf ball and flatten in the palm of your hands to form small patties. You should get about 10–12 patties.

If the patty mixture seems to break apart easily, add about 1 tablespoon of plain flour to the mixture to help the patties stay together.

Once you have made the lentil patties, heat the oil in a frying pan, add the patties in batches and fry over a medium heat, turning them at least once.

Serve these Lentil and Vegetable Patties hot.

Sambhar

A typical South Indian lentil dish that is probably made every day in most South Indian homes. It can also be made using masoor dhaal (split red lentils), urid dhaal, or a mixture of chickpeas and urid dhaal. Vary the lentil variety according to taste.

175 G (6 OZ) TOOR DHAAL
1½ TEASPOONS GROUND CORIANDER
¼ TEASPOON TURMERIC
1½ TEASPOONS CHILLI POWDER
¼ TEASPOON GROUND FENUGREEK
900 ML (1½ PINTS) WATER
6 SMALL CAULIFLOWER FLORETS
125 G (4 OZ) FROZEN GREEN BEANS
2 TOMATOES, QUARTERED
2 GREEN CHILLIES, CHOPPED
1½ TEASPOONS SALT
6 BABY ONIONS, PEELED
1 TABLESPOON TAMARIND PASTE
1 TABLESPOON BROWN SUGAR
FOR THE BAGHAAR TARICA
4 TABLESPOONS CORN OIL
¼ TEASPOON MUSTARD SEEDS
6 WHOLE CURRY LEAVES
A LARGE PINCH OF WHITE CUMIN SEEDS
4 DRIED RED CHILLIES
3 GARLIC CLOVES
A PINCH OF ASAFOETIDA
FRESH CORIANDER, TO GARNISH

Wash the toor dhaal, place in a heavy-based saucepan and add the ground coriander, turmeric, chilli powder, fenugreek and water. Cover the pan and cook the mixture over a medium heat, stirring occasionally to prevent it overflowing.

Once the toor dhaal is soft enough to be mashed, mash it down in the saucepan. If the dhaal is too thick, add another 150 ml (¼ pint) of water to loosen the consistency.

Next, add the cauliflower, beans, tomatoes, green chillies, salt, baby onions, tamarind paste and brown sugar and bring to the boil. Lower the heat and simmer gently for a further 10 minutes. Adjust the consistency and seasoning to taste. Transfer to a serving dish and set aside.

Meanwhile, make the baghaar tarica. Heat the oil in a frying pan, add the mustard seeds, curry leaves, cumin seeds, dried red chillies, garlic and asafoetida and fry until everything turns a shade darker. Pour the hot baghaar over the toor dhaal.

Serve garnished with the fresh coriander.

Bitter Gourds with Chana Dhaal
(Karela Dhaal)

Karela, or bitter gourd, is a vegetable with a very distinctive bitter taste. You prepare it as you would cucumber for cooking. Cut in half lengthways, scoop out the seeds and sprinkle the flesh with salt to draw out some of the bitter juices before cooking. Alternatively, just take off the rough part of the skin, leaving the seeds in, then chop the flesh into large dice before salting. Delicious and delicate with dhaal.

2 BITTER GOURDS, ABOUT 13 CM (5 INCHES) LONG
1 TABLESPOON SALT
125 G (4 OZ) CHANA DHAAL
2 ONIONS, SLICED
1 TEASPOON GINGER PULP
1 TEASPOON CHILLI POWDER
1 TEASPOON GARLIC PULP
1 TEASPOON GARAM MASALA
1 TEASPOON GROUND CORIANDER
1½ TEASPOONS SALT
600 ML (1 PINT) WATER
4 TABLESPOONS CORN OIL
2 TOMATOES, SLICED
TO GARNISH
1 X 2.5 CM (1 INCH) PIECE FRESH GINGER, SHREDDED
½ TEASPOON GARAM MASALA
1 TABLESPOON FRESH CORIANDER
1 GREEN CHILLI, SLICED

Wash the bitter gourds and pat dry with kitchen paper. Peel off the rough skins and slice the gourds, discarding the seeds. Place the sliced gourds in a bowl, rubbing the tablespoon of salt into the slices. Set aside for about 1 hour.

Meanwhile, wash the chana dhaal and place in a saucepan. Add 1 of the sliced onions, the ginger, chilli powder, garlic, garam masala, ground coriander, salt and water and cook over a medium heat, partly covered, for 15–20 minutes or until the dhaal is soft but not mushy, and all the water has been absorbed. Remove from the heat and set aside.

Wash the bitter gourds thoroughly to remove all the salt and add to the dhaal.

Heat the corn oil in a deep frying pan and fry the remaining sliced onion until golden brown. Add the sliced tomatoes and the dhaal and stir-fry for about 3 minutes to blend together.

Transfer to a serving dish and serve garnished with shredded ginger, garam masala, fresh coriander and sliced green chillies.

This dish goes well with hot chapatis or puris.

Illustrated on page 77.

84

Masala Urid Dhaal

Urid is a small lentil with a black skin, closely related to moong dhaal. There are two varieties of urid dhaal – the skinned kind, which are creamy-white in colour, and the unskinned kind, with black husks, split, so they show their pale interiors. The type of urid lentil used in this recipe is the whole one with the husks removed. It is readily available in all Asian supermarkets.

250 G (8 OZ) URID DHAAL

2 TABLESPOONS PURE GHEE

1 LARGE ONION, SLICED

1 X 3.5 CM (1½ INCH) PIECE FRESH GINGER, SHREDDED

4 GARLIC CLOVES, SLICED

2 GREEN CHILLIES, SLICED

2 RED CHILLIES, SLICED

½ TEASPOON ONION SEEDS

1 TABLESPOON LEMON JUICE

1 TABLESPOON CHOPPED FRESH CORIANDER

1 TABLESPOON FRESH MINT

MASALA

½ TEASPOON GROUND CUMIN

½ TEASPOON GROUND CORIANDER

½ TEASPOON BLACK SALT

¼ TEASPOON CITRIC ACID

Boil the lentils in 600 ml (1 pint) of lightly salted water until soft but not mushy. Drain and place in a serving dish.

Melt the ghee in a frying pan over a high heat, add the onion and fry until golden brown. Lower the heat to medium and add the ginger, garlic, green and red chillies, onion seeds and lemon juice, stirring constantly.

Pour the mixture over the dhaal in the serving dish and garnish with the fresh coriander and mint.

Mix the masala ingredients together in a small bowl and sprinkle over the dhaal.

Serve with freshly made chapatis.

Spicy Chickpeas
(Chana Masala)

This recipe uses canned chickpeas, which I find is a much more convenient way of using this delicious pulse, rather than starting from the beginning with dried ones. If you prefer to use the dried ones however, soak them in the usual way – in cold water for at least 12 hours or overnight. It is a good idea to change the soaking water several times during this period if possible. When soaked, drain the chickpeas and, for about 500 g (1 lb) dry weight, cover with 2 litres (3½ pints) cold water. Bring to the boil, skim the froth off the top, then simmer for 2–3 hours, or until tender. Add salt about half way through the cooking time.

2 ONIONS, CHOPPED

1½ TEASPOONS GARAM MASALA

1 TEASPOON CHILLI POWDER

2 TEASPOONS GROUND POMEGRANATE SEEDS

½ TEASPOON GARLIC PULP

1 TEASPOON SALT

2 TABLESPOONS TOMATO PURÉE

3 TABLESPOONS CORN OIL

2 GARLIC CLOVES

1 X 2.5 CM (1 INCH) PIECE FRESH GINGER, SHREDDED

½ TEASPOON WHITE CUMIN SEEDS

1 X 475 G (15 OZ) CAN CHICKPEAS, DRAINED

TO GARNISH

1 TABLESPOON CHOPPED FRESH CORIANDER

2 TOMATOES, SLICED

2 GREEN CHILLIES, SLICED

1 SMALL ONION, SLICED IN RINGS

Place the onions in a food processor with the garam masala, chilli powder, ground pomegranate seeds, garlic, salt and tomato purée and blend for about 20 seconds.

Heat the oil in a karahi or deep frying pan, add the garlic cloves and shredded ginger and fry for about 10 seconds before adding the cumin seeds. Fry these for 10 seconds, lower the heat and add the onion mixture to the pan.

Stir-fry for about 3 minutes to cook the spices, then add the chickpeas. Continue to cook for a further 5–7 minutes.

Transfer the dhaal to a serving dish and garnish with the fresh coriander, sliced tomato, green chillies and onion rings.

Spicy Tomatoes and Aubergines with Chickpeas

Chickpeas are a favourite ingredient in Middle Eastern and Mediterranean cooking, as well as Indian. There, too, they are teamed with tomatoes and aubergines, which just goes to emphasize that some ingredients seem made for each other. Chickpeas are a very good source of protein for vegetarians and they become a beautiful golden yellow when cooked, making this a colourful and attractive dish for entertaining.

5 TABLESPOONS CORN OIL

1 ONION, DICED

1 TEASPOON GINGER PULP

¼ TEASPOON TURMERIC

1 TEASPOON GARLIC PULP

1 TEASPOON GARAM MASALA

1½ TEASPOONS GROUND CORIANDER

1 TEASPOON CHILLI POWDER

1 X 425 G (14 OZ) CAN TOMATOES

1 SMALL AUBERGINE, DICED

1 ORANGE PEPPER, DESEEDED AND DICED

250 G (8 OZ) CANNED CHICKPEAS, DRAINED

1–1½ TEASPOONS SALT

Heat the corn oil in a karahi or deep frying pan, add the diced onion and fry until golden brown. Lower the heat and stir in the ginger, turmeric, garlic, garam masala, ground coriander and chilli powder.

Pour in the tomatoes and their juice, then the aubergine, orange pepper, chickpeas and salt to taste. Stir-fry for about 5–7 minutes, trying not to break the chickpeas.

Serve hot with a rice dish.

VARIATIONS

Substitute black-eye beans, dried butter beans or dried haricot or flageolet beans for the chickpeas. If you would prefer to use dried chickpeas rather than canned, prepare the dried ones as described in the introduction to the recipe on page 85.

Spicy Black-eye Beans
(Masala Lobia)

Black-eye beans have a wonderful earthy flavour and excellent texture. Also known as black-eyed peas, they are a variety of cow peas, and are widely used in Caribbean and Southern American cooking. They are easily identified by the distinctive black 'eye' on top of the cream kidney-shaped bean. Although black-eye beans are quite widely available, you could also make this dish with dried or canned haricot beans or butter beans.

175 G (6 OZ) BLACK-EYE BEANS

5 TABLESPOONS CORN OIL

2 ONIONS, SLICED

1 TEASPOON GINGER PULP

1 TEASPOON GROUND CORIANDER

1½ TEASPOONS CHILLI POWDER

½ TEASPOON TURMERIC

2 TOMATOES, CHOPPED

½ TEASPOON SALT

2 TABLESPOONS LEMON JUICE

2 GREEN CHILLIES

TO GARNISH

300 ML (½ PINT) OIL

8–10 BABY POTATOES, SLICED

1 TABLESPOON CHOPPED FRESH MINT

1 TEASPOON GARAM MASALA

Wash the black-eye beans and cook in boiling water until soft. Drain and set aside.

Heat the corn oil in a large frying pan, add the sliced onions and fry until golden brown. Lower the heat and add the ginger, coriander, chilli powder, turmeric, chopped tomatoes and salt. Stir-fry for about 2 minutes.

Carefully tip in the black-eye beans and blend together. Add the lemon juice and green chillies, stir to mix and transfer to a serving dish.

For the garnish, heat the oil in a deep frying pan to 190°C (375°F), or until a cube of bread browns in 30 seconds, add the potato slices and fry until cooked. Arrange the potato slices on top of the black-eye beans and garnish the dish with the mint. Sprinkle the garam masala over the top before serving.

RIGHT: *From top, two easily prepared pulse dishes, Spicy Black-eye Beans – Masala Lobia – (recipe above, right) and Spicy Tomatoes and Aubergines with Chickpeas (recipe above).*

Black-eye Beans

Black-eye beans cook very quickly, and do not require pre-soaking – an excellent ingredient to choose for a quick meal. The slightly smoky, earthy flavour of these beans goes very well with vegetables such as aubergines and tomatoes, and so do chickpeas, as shown in the variation below.

250 G (8 OZ) BLACK-EYE BEANS
4 TABLESPOONS CORN OIL
1 ONION, CHOPPED
1 TEASPOON CHILLI POWDER
3 TABLESPOONS LEMON JUICE
1½ TEASPOONS GROUND CORIANDER
1½ TEASPOONS SALT
3 TABLESPOONS CHOPPED FRESH CORIANDER
3 GREEN CHILLIES
2 TOMATOES, SLICED
1 LEMON, SLICED

Wash the black-eye beans and boil in plenty of water until soft. Drain and set aside in a bowl.

Heat the oil in a heavy-based saucepan, add the chopped onion and fry over a medium heat. Lower the heat then add the chilli powder, lemon juice, ground coriander and salt. Pour in the black-eye beans and stir-fry. Turn the heat off, then cover and set aside.

Place the fresh coriander and the green chillies in a food processor and blend for 30 seconds.

Transfer the beans to a serving dish and mix in the green chillies and coriander mixture.

Garnish with the sliced tomatoes and lemon slices and serve.

VARIATION
Chickpeas with Aubergines
Substitute a similar quantity of canned chickpeas for the black-eye beans and add 1 aubergine as well as the tomatoes. Slice the aubergine, sprinkle with salt to drain out the bitter juices. Set aside for 30 minutes, then rinse and pat dry. Proceed as in the main recipe.

Dried chickpeas may also be used. Before using them in this recipe, soak them in cold water overnight, changing the water several times if possible, then cook in the following way.

Place the chickpeas in a saucepan with cold water to cover. Bring to the boil and skim the foam which rises to the surface. Reduce the heat and simmer gently for 2–3 hours (the length of time will depend on the age of the chickpeas). Add salt about halfway through the cooking time. Drain, then proceed as in the main recipe.

Baby Potatoes with Haricot Beans

Haricot beans are not widely used in Indian cooking, although they marry perfectly with these spices and aromatics. Like so many other interesting vegetables, they were introduced to Europe from North America in the 16th Century, and enthusiastically adopted by the French. Haricots are very nutritious and contain more protein than meat, so are very valuable in a vegetarian diet. Flageolet beans were developed from them in the middle of the last century, and could also be used in this recipe; they are available canned or dried.

15 BABY POTATOES
125 G (4 OZ) HARICOT BEANS, CANNED OR FROZEN
250 ML (8 FL OZ) NATURAL YOGURT
1 TEASPOON GINGER PULP
1 TEASPOON GARLIC PULP
1 TABLESPOON TOMATO PURÉE
1½ TEASPOONS GARAM MASALA
1 TEASPOON CHILLI POWDER
1 TEASPOON SALT
½ TEASPOON GROUND FENNEL SEEDS
4 TABLESPOONS OIL
2 BAY LEAVES
1 LARGE ONION, DICED
2 TABLESPOONS CHOPPED FRESH CORIANDER
2 TOMATOES, QUARTERED

Boil the baby potatoes in lightly salted water until cooked, drain and set aside. Drain or thaw the haricot beans, depending on which kind you are using.

In a mixing bowl, mix the yogurt, ginger, garlic, tomato purée, garam masala, chilli powder, salt and ground fennel seeds. Mix together thoroughly and set aside.

Heat the oil in a medium-sized saucepan, add the bay leaves and onion and fry for about 5 minutes over a medium heat.

Stir the yogurt and spice mixture into the onions and stir-fry for 3–5 minutes, or until the sauce has thickened. Add the potatoes and beans and half the fresh coriander. Continue to stir-fry gently, trying not to break up the vegetables.

Once the sauce has thickened and has a semi-dry texture, stir in the remaining fresh coriander and quartered tomatoes.

Cook for a further 2 minutes over a low heat and serve hot with puris.

VARIATION
This recipe can also be made with dried white haricot beans or green flageolets. Soak in water overnight, drain, then cover with cold water, bring to the boil and simmer until tender. Proceed as in the main recipe.

Broad Beans with Spring Onions

I suggest you cook this dish in butter. Though broad beans are not widely used in India, they are delicious this way.

2 TABLESPOONS BUTTER

1 TABLESPOON CORN OIL

½ TEASPOON ONION SEEDS

3 BUNCHES SPRING ONIONS, CHOPPED

3 RED CHILLIES, CHOPPED ROUGHLY

1 GREEN PEPPER, SLICED

½ TEASPOON GARLIC

½ TEASPOON GINGER

1 TEASPOON CHILLI POWDER

1 TABLESPOON LEMON JUICE

1 X 475 G (15 OZ) CAN BROAD BEANS, DRAINED

175 G (6 OZ) MUSHROOMS, SLICED

2 TABLESPOONS FRESH CORIANDER

1 TEASPOON SALT

Heat the butter with 1 tablespoon of oil and fry the onion seeds for 30 seconds, add the spring onions and fry until soft.

Add half the red chillies, green pepper, garlic, ginger, chilli powder and lemon juice to the pan. Stir-fry for 2 minutes then lower the heat, add the broad beans and stir-fry.

Next add the mushrooms, coriander and salt. Stir in the remaining red chillies, stir-fry for 3–5 minutes and serve hot.

Chohlay

This is a very popular snack or part of a vegetarian meal.

1 X 475 G (15 OZ) CAN CHICKPEAS, DRAINED

1 LARGE POTATO, CUBED AND BOILED

2 TEASPOONS POMEGRANATE SEEDS

1 TEASPOON SUGAR

2 TABLESPOONS LEMON JUICE

1 TEASPOON GROUND CORIANDER

½ TEASPOON GARAM MASALA

1 TEASPOON CHILLI POWDER

1 ONION, FINELY DICED

2 GREEN CHILLIES

1 TABLESPOON FRESH CORIANDER

2 TOMATOES

Put the chickpeas and potato in a bowl. Roast the pomegranate seeds and grind in a spice grinder. Mix the seeds with sugar, lemon juice, coriander, garam masala and chilli powder. Then pour over the chickpeas; mix well. Add the onion, garnish with green chillies, coriander and tomato. Serve hot or cold.

Baby Corn and Mushrooms with Moong Dhaal

Vegetables such as corn, native to the Americas, were unknown in India until introduced by the Portuguese, probably in the 16th Century. Corn and other New World vegetables have been enthusiastically adopted there, as in Europe. Baby corn is widely available in supermarkets and oriental delicatessens and is fresh and delicious in this stir-fried lentil dish.

50 G (2 OZ) MOONG DHAAL

4 TABLESPOONS CORN OIL

2 ONIONS, DICED

1 TEASPOON GROUND CORIANDER

2 TEASPOONS MANGO POWDER

1 TEASPOON CHILLI POWDER

¼ TEASPOON TURMERIC

1 TEASPOON SALT

175 G (6 OZ) BABY CORN

75 G (3 OZ) FROZEN PEAS

250 G (8 OZ) MUSHROOMS

Boil the moong dhaal in lightly salted water until soft but not mushy. Drain, place in a bowl and set aside.

Heat the oil in a heavy-based saucepan, add the diced onions and fry until golden brown.

Meanwhile, mix together the ground coriander, with the mango powder, chilli powder, turmeric and salt in a small bowl and pour the mixture into the fried onions. Lower the heat immediately and stir-fry for about 1 minute.

Add the baby corn, peas and mushrooms and continue to stir-fry for a further 3–5 minutes.

Mix in the moong dhaal and serve immediately, accompanied by freshly made paratas (see recipe on page 103).

89

Rice

The ideal rice for Indian dishes is Basmati – a fine, long-grained rice with a delicate perfume. Basmati rice must be picked over, washed and well drained before use. This process is not necessary with a packaged American rice, though it will have a better texture if it is washed.

Aromatic Rice

Rice is the basis of most Indian meals, vegetarian or otherwise, especially in the south. Basmati is the variety most highly regarded, but it can be very delicate, and should be handled carefully during cooking. Because the rice itself is the focal point of this dish I think it is worth using the very best quality you can find. If Basmati is not available, any other good, long-grained rice could be substituted, including Patna, or American long-grained rice. When preparing rice, you must always wash it in several changes of cold water, until it runs clear. This will rinse away the cloudy starch particles, which would otherwise make the rice sticky. This rice is very simple to cook and is made using only whole spices. Use the same sized cup to measure the rice and the water.

2 CUPS BASMATI RICE

125 G (4 OZ) UNSALTED BUTTER

1 TABLESPOON CORN OIL

1 TEASPOON MUSTARD SEEDS

4 WHOLE DRIED RED CHILLIES

6 CURRY LEAVES

1 X 3.5 CM (1½ INCH) PIECE OF
FRESH GINGER, SHREDDED

3 GARLIC CLOVES, SLICED

1 TEASPOON SALT

3 CUPS WATER

Wash the rice until the water runs clear, drain and set aside.

Melt the butter and oil in a heavy-based saucepan over a medium heat, add the mustard seeds, dried red chillies, curry leaves, ginger, garlic and salt and fry for about 2 minutes.

Add the rice and stir-fry gently for a further minute, then pour in the water. Increase the heat and bring to the boil. Lower the heat to medium, cover the saucepan and cook for 15 minutes, or until the rice is tender and all the water has been absorbed.

Let the rice stand for about 5 minutes before serving.

Fried Rice with Cashew Nuts

The cashew nut, which is now used in so many Indian dishes, is not native to Asia. Like so many interesting ingredients, it came to Europe from South America after the voyage of Columbus. The Portuguese probably introduced it to India, and it is a very important crop in the old Portuguese colony of Goa on the west coast. There, the trees grow wild as well as being cultivated, and the nut is even used to produce a very fiery, vodka-like spirit called 'feni' – very much an acquired taste! In this recipe, as in all the others in this chapter, use the same sized cup for measuring the Basmati rice and the water.

3 CUPS BASMATI RICE

2 TABLESPOONS GHEE

4 WHOLE CLOVES

4 WHOLE CARDAMOMS

2 WHOLE BAY LEAVES

1 TEASPOON SALT

1 GREEN CHILLI, SLICED

2 RED CHILLIES, SLICED

25 G (1 OZ) CASHEW NUTS

25 G (1 OZ) SULTANAS

4 CUPS WATER

Wash the rice and set it aside to drain.

Melt the ghee in a heavy-based saucepan or a deep frying pan with a lid, add the whole cloves, cardamoms, bay leaves, salt, green and red chillies and fry over a medium heat for about 2–3 minutes. Lower the heat and add the cashew nuts and the sultanas.

Using a slotted spoon, stir in the rice and stir-fry for about 2 minutes. Pour in the water and bring to the boil. Lower the heat, cover the pan and cook for 15–20 minutes, or until the rice is tender and the water has been absorbed.

This rice dish is best served with a creamy curry.

PREVIOUS PAGES: *From left, Cabbage and Carrot Pulao (recipe page 98) and Fried Rice with Cashew Nuts (recipe above, right). Pulaos are one of the finest of all rice dishes and are typical of the Moghul influence in Indian cooking. Use Basmati rice wherever possible in the dishes in this chapter – its quality is, without doubt, the best available.*

Bay Rice
(Tez Pattay Kay Chawal)

A recipe using European bay leaves. They are a different species from the Indian variety however. European bay leaves come from a tree which is a species of laurel, whereas the Indian variety comes from the cassia tree, and has a mysterious cinnamon-like scent. You could also try it with Indian bay leaves, which are widely available in Asian food stores, as is the bark of the same tree. Use the same sized cup to measure the rice and the water in this recipe.

2 CUPS BASMATI RICE

75 G (3 OZ) BUTTER

1 TABLESPOON OIL

½ TEASPOON WHITE CUMIN SEEDS

3 CLOVES

6–8 BLACK PEPPERCORNS

4 GREEN CARDAMOMS

2 BAY LEAVES

1 TEASPOON SALT

3 CUPS WATER

Wash the rice, drain and set aside. Melt the butter with the oil in a heavy-based saucepan, add the white cumin seeds, cloves, peppercorns, cardamoms and bay leaves and fry over a medium heat for 1–2 minutes.

Add the salt and rice to the saucepan and stir-fry gently for about 1 minute, then pour in the water. Turn the heat to high and bring to the boil, reduce the heat to medium, cover the pan and cook for 15–20 minutes, or until the rice is tender and the water has been absorbed.

Let the rice stand in the pan for 5 minutes before serving.

VARIATION
Bay Rice with Shredded Ginger
Ginger makes an interesting variation for this recipe. Peel 2.5 cm (1 inch) of fresh root ginger and shred finely. Add together with the other spices and proceed as in the main recipe.

Rice Cooked with Spring Onions

The proportion of rice to water is crucial in rice cooking so always use the same sized cup to measure rice and water.

2 CUPS BASMATI RICE

75 G (3 OZ) BUTTER

1 TABLESPOON CORN OIL

½ TEASPOON FENNEL SEEDS

½ TEASPOON GINGER PULP

½ TEASPOON GARLIC PULP

1 TEASPOON SALT

1 LARGE RED PEPPER, DESEEDED AND DICED

2 SMALL BUNCHES SPRING ONIONS, CHOPPED

3 CUPS WATER

Wash the rice, drain into a strainer and set aside.

Heat the butter and oil in a heavy-based saucepan over a medium heat, add the fennel seeds, ginger, garlic and salt and stir-fry for 1 minute.

Add half the red pepper and all the spring onions and stir-fry over a medium heat for about 2 minutes.

Stir the rice in and stir-fry gently for about 1 minute.

Pour the water in and bring to the boil, lower the heat to medium, cover the saucepan and cook for 15–20 minutes, or until the rice is tender and the water has been absorbed.

Remove the lid to check if the rice is cooked and stir in the remaining diced pepper before serving.

Idlis

Light, fluffy rice cakes, popular as a breakfast dish with a knob of butter and honey or jam (not traditional, but wonderful!) – also delicious with curry sauces, dhaals, or spicy raitas. Steam them in patty pans, or dariole moulds.

150 G (5 OZ) URID DHAAL

1 TEASPOON SALT

375 G (12 OZ) PARBOILED RICE

CORN OIL, FOR GREASING

Soak the urid dhaal for 1 hour, drain and place in a liquidizer or food processor with the salt. Blend to a paste.

Grind the rice to a coarse powder, place in muslin and rinse carefully. Set aside to soak for 10–15 minutes, then squeeze out the excess moisture and mix with the lentil paste. Set aside in a warm place for 6 hours or overnight.

Grease the patty pans, spoon in the rice and lentil mixture, then steam over boiling water for about 10 minutes. Pierce with a skewer; the idlis are cooked when it comes out clean.

Vegetable Biryani

The 'home' of the biryani is Hyderabad in south-central India – one of the great Moghul cities, which still has a very large Muslim population. This is one of the elegant dishes the Moghuls brought with them – the product of the very sophisticated cooking of the courts of great emperors such as Akbar, Jehangir and Shah Jahan, who built the Taj Mahal as the tomb for his wife, Mumtaz. Though Moghul recipes like this were usually made with fish, chicken or lamb, the vegetarian version is equally splendid. Instead of covering the pan with foil, then the lid, Moghul cooks would have sealed it with a ring of dough, with the lid on top, in much the same way as French 'daubes' are. Biryanis are cooked for special occasions, and the method is very interesting as the rice and vegetables are layered and saffron soaked in milk is poured over the top to make the rice partly coloured. This recipe will serve six, with accompaniments.

2 ONIONS, SLICED

1 AUBERGINE, CUT INTO 6–8 PIECES

2 CARROTS, SLICED

½ CAULIFLOWER, CUT INTO SMALL FLORETS

75 G (3 OZ) FRENCH BEANS,
CUT INTO 2.5 CM (1 INCH) PIECES

75 G (3 OZ) FROZEN PEAS

5 TABLESPOONS VEGETABLE GHEE

6 CARDAMOMS

4 WHOLE CLOVES

2 WHOLE CINNAMON STICKS

75 G (3 OZ) SULTANAS

75 G (3 OZ) CASHEW NUTS

250 G (8 OZ) NATURAL YOGURT

1½ TEASPOONS FRESH GINGER PULP

1½ TEASPOONS FRESH GARLIC PULP

1 TEASPOON BLACK CUMIN SEEDS

1 TEASPOON GARAM MASALA

2 TEASPOONS SALT

50 G (2 OZ) GROUND ALMONDS

750 G (1½ LB) BASMATI RICE

1.5 LITRES (2½ PINTS) WATER

4 TABLESPOONS CHOPPED FRESH CORIANDER

5 TABLESPOONS LEMON JUICE

3 GREEN CHILLIES, CHOPPED

1–2 TEASPOONS SAFFRON STRANDS,
CRUSHED AND SOAKED IN
150 ML (¼ PINT) MILK

Wash and prepare all the vegetables. In a large saucepan heat the ghee, add the onions and fry until golden brown. Using a slotted spoon, remove half the onions and set aside in a bowl together with half the ghee.

Now add half of the whole spices – that is, the 3 cardamoms, 2 cloves and 1 cinnamon stick – and all the vegetables to the remaining onions and fry them until soft. Add the sultanas and cashew nuts.

Meanwhile, in a separate bowl mix the yogurt, ginger, garlic, cumin seeds, garam masala, half of the salt and half the ground almonds. Pour this mixture over the the vegetables and continue to stir-fry for a further 7–10 minutes. Remove the pan from the heat and set aside.

Wash the Basmati rice at least twice, handling it gently, then set aside to drain.

Into a large saucepan pour the measured water along with the remaining salt, half the fresh coriander and the remaining black cumin seeds, cloves, cardamoms and cinnamon stick. Bring to the boil. Drain off any water from the rice in the bowl and transfer the rice to the boiling water in the saucepan. Bring to the boil and part-cook the rice. To check whether it is part-cooked, press a few grains between your thumb and forefinger. The rice should be soft on top and hard in the middle. Immediately the rice reaches this stage, drain it through a strainer. Divide the rice equally, leaving half in the strainer and spooning half into a saucepan.

Pour all the vegetable mixture over the top of the rice in the saucepan and garnish with half the fried onions, ghee, fresh coriander, lemon juice and half the green chillies.

Cover with the remaining rice, pour over the saffron in milk and garnish with the remaining ingredients.

Cover the saucepan first with foil and then with a tight-fitting lid. Return the saucepan to the heat and cook over a medium heat for 15–20 minutes, checking once to see that the rice is cooked right through. Leave to stand for 10–15 minutes. Mix gently with a slotted spoon before serving. A raita is usually served to complement the biryani, and at a dinner party, you could add a crunchy salad, such as Tomato and Onion Salad on page 111 or the Grated Mooli Salad on page 113. Serve also with crisp poppadums and a good, thick dhaal, such as Rasam or Toor Dhaal with Tomatoes, both on page 82.

VARIATION

A biryani can also be given the final cooking layered in a large bowl and cooked in a moderate oven. Once cooked, it can be turned out on to a dish as a mould.

RIGHT: *From top, the elegant, special-occasion Vegetable Biryani (recipe above) together with the curry dish, Vegetables in a Tangy Sauce (recipe page 38). Biryanis are yet another of the wonderful dishes introduced into India by the Moghuls.*

Rice and Peas in Green Spices

(Haray Masalay Kay Chawal)

'Chawal' means, simply, 'plain rice', and is complemented here by peas and mint. It is astonishing how the same 'marriages' of ingredients occur in many different cuisines. In Italian cooking, for instance, one of the great classics is 'risi e bisi' (rice and peas). Peas are often cooked with mint in both French and English cooking. Use the same cup to measure the rice and the water in this recipe.

2 CUPS BASMATI RICE

3 TABLESPOONS PURE GHEE

1 LARGE BUNCH SPRING ONIONS, CHOPPED

1 TEASPOON GINGER PULP

1 TEASPOON GARLIC PULP

½ TEASPOON WHITE CUMIN SEEDS

3–4 GREEN CARDAMOMS, WHOLE

3 GREEN CHILLIES, CHOPPED

2 TABLESPOONS CHOPPED FRESH CORIANDER

1 TABLESPOON CHOPPED FRESH MINT LEAVES

50 G (2 OZ) FROZEN PEAS

3 TABLESPOONS NATURAL YOGURT

2 TEASPOONS SALT

3 CUPS WATER

Wash the rice at least twice, drain off the water and set the rice aside in a bowl.

Heat the ghee in a medium-sized saucepan, add the spring onions and fry for about 2 minutes before adding the ginger, garlic, white cumin seeds, green cardamoms, green chillies, fresh coriander, mint and frozen peas. Lower the heat and stir-fry for a further 2 minutes. Stir in the yogurt and continue to stir-fry for another 2 minutes.

Add the rice and stir to mix together. Add the salt, pour in the water, bring to the boil, lower the heat to medium, cover the pan and cook for 15–20 minutes, or until the rice is tender and the water has been absorbed.

Let the rice stand for 5–7 minutes before serving with any of the curries in this book.

Vegetable Rice

(Subzee Kay Chacoal)

When serving this or other rice dishes with the curries in this book, always allow the rice to stand for about 5 minutes before serving.

4 TABLESPOONS OIL

8 CURRY LEAVES

6 GREEN CHILLIES, CHOPPED

1 ONION, SLICED

2 TOMATOES

½ TEASPOON GINGER PULP

½ TEASPOON GARLIC PULP

½ TEASPOON DRIED RED CHILLIES

½ TEASPOON TURMERIC

1 POTATO, DICED

1 CARROT, DICED

2 TABLESPOONS MOONG DHAAL

2 CUPS RICE

2 TEASPOONS SALT

3 CUPS WATER

4–6 TABLESPOONS LEMON JUICE

2 TABLESPOONS CHOPPED FRESH CORIANDER

Heat the oil in a heavy-based saucepan, add the curry leaves and green chillies, and fry for 2 minutes. Add the onion and fry for 2–3 minutes over a medium heat. Gradually add the tomatoes, ginger, garlic, dried red chillies, turmeric, diced potato, carrots and moong dhaal.

Once all the ingredients are blended, continue stir-frying, reducing the heat if necessary, for 2–3 minutes.

Now pour the rice in and continue to stir-fry the mixture in semi-circular movements.

Pour in the salt, water, lemon juice and fresh coriander and stir to mix together. Bring to the boil, lower the heat, cover the pan and cook for 15–20 minutes, or until the rice is tender and the water has been absorbed,

Leave the rice to stand for 5–7 minutes before serving.

Saffron Rice with Peas
(Zafraan Aur Majar Pulao)

Saffron is one of the ingredients that indicates a Moghul origin in an Indian dish. It is made from the stigmas of the saffron crocus, which must be laboriously removed from the blossoms by hand – and this makes it a very expensive spice indeed. Some people substitute turmeric, but the only similarity will be the yellow colour – the flavour is quite different, and the colour is rather more 'mustardy' than the clear golden orange of true saffron. In this dish, the saffron is poured in at the end, so the yellow appears as seams through the rice. This rice dish is garnished with delicious, crisp, golden-brown onions and fresh coriander.
Remember to use the same cup to measure the rice and the water.

2 TABLESPOONS PURE GHEE

2 ONIONS, SLICED

1 TEASPOON WHITE CUMIN SEEDS

3 BLACK CARDAMOMS

1 X 3.5 CM (1½ INCH) PIECE CINNAMON STICK

2 CUPS RICE

50 G (2 OZ) PEAS

1½ TEASPOONS SALT

3 CUPS WATER

4 TABLESPOONS MILK

½ TEASPOON SAFFRON STRANDS, CRUSHED

1 TABLESPOON CHOPPED FRESH CORIANDER

Melt the ghee in a heavy-based saucepan over a high heat, add the onions and fry until crisp and golden brown.

Transfer half the onions into a bowl and reserve for garnish.

Lower the heat and add the whole spices to the saucepan, followed by the washed rice, peas and salt, stirring gently with a slotted spoon.

Pour in the water and bring to the boil. Lower the heat, cover the pan and cook for 15–20 minutes, or until the rice is tender and the water has been absorbed.

Meanwhile, heat the milk and add the saffron strands.

When the rice is cooked, pour the saffron milk over it and let the rice stand for a further 5 minutes before serving garnished with the crisp onions and fresh coriander.

Pea Pulao
(Majar Pulao)

Pulaos, like biryanis, were introduced to India by the Moghuls, and this method of cooking is one favoured by them, called 'dum'. Dum cooking is a little like the French 'daube', which can be cooked in the oven or on top of the stove – as long as the cooking vessel is tightly closed after the rice is brought to the boil. In this way, the ingredients are steamed to tenderness.

1 TABLESPOON CORN OIL

125 G (4 OZ) UNSALTED BUTTER

1 ONION, SLICED

3 WHOLE BLACK CARDAMOMS

6 WHOLE CLOVES

¼ TEASPOON BLACK CUMIN SEEDS

6–8 WHOLE BLACK PEPPERCORNS

1 TEASPOON GINGER PULP

1 TEASPOON GARLIC PULP

2 WHOLE BAY LEAVES

2 CINNAMON STICKS

125 G (4 OZ) NATURAL YOGURT

75 G (3 OZ) PEAS

3 POTATOES, CUT INTO WEDGES

1 TABLESPOON CHOPPED FRESH CORIANDER

2 GREEN CHILLIES, SLICED

2 CUPS BASMATI RICE

1 TEASPOON SALT

3 CUPS WATER

Heat the oil and butter in a medium-sized saucepan. Add the onion, black cardamoms, whole cloves, black cumin seeds and black peppercorns and fry until the onions are golden brown. Add the ginger, garlic, bay leaves and cinnamon sticks.

Meanwhile, whisk the natural yogurt lightly and pour on to the onions, followed by the peas and potatoes.

Stir-fry the mixture for a further 3 minutes, then pour in the remaining ingredients, except the water. Using a slotted spoon, mix the rice in gently, then stir-fry for about 2 minutes.

Pour in the water. Increase the heat to high and bring to the boil. Lower the heat to medium, cover the saucepan and cook for 15–20 minutes, or until the rice is tender and the water has been absorbed.

Let the rice stand for 5–7 minutes before serving.

Pea and Sweetcorn Pulao
(Matar Aur Bhutta Ka Pulao)

Biryanis and pulaos always make wonderful party dishes, as they can be prepared early in the day and covered with foil until needed. Place them in a preheated oven at about 190°C (375°F), Gas Mark 5 for about 25–30 minutes before serving.

2 CUPS BASMATI RICE

3 TABLESPOONS GHEE

½ TEASPOON BLACK CUMIN SEEDS

6–8 BLACK PEPPERCORNS

3 WHOLE CLOVES

3 GREEN CARDAMOMS

1 X 2.5 CM (1 INCH) PIECE
CINNAMON STICK, CUT IN HALF

1 ONION, DICED

1½ TABLESPOONS SALT

1 TABLESPOON CHOPPED FRESH CORIANDER

2 GREEN CHILLIES, CHOPPED

2 BAY LEAVES

1 POTATO, DICED

125 G (4 OZ) PEAS

50 G (2 OZ) SWEETCORN

3 CUPS WATER

TOMATO SLICES, TO GARNISH (OPTIONAL)

Wash the rice, drain and set aside.

Heat the ghee in a heavy-based saucepan, add the cumin seeds, black peppercorns, cloves, cardamoms and cinnamon and fry for about 30–40 seconds before adding the onion. Continue frying until the onion is golden brown.

Add the salt, coriander, green chillies, bay leaves, potatoes, peas and sweetcorn. Stir-fry for 3–5 minutes.

Mix in the rice, followed by the water. Bring to the boil, lower the heat, cover the pan and cook for 15–20 minutes, or until the rice is tender and the water has been absorbed.

Leave the rice to stand for a further 5 minutes before serving garnished with sliced tomatoes, if liked.

VARIATION
Pea and Sweetcorn Pulao with Saffron
Soak a pinch of saffron strands in a little milk, then pour over the pulao. Alternatively, mix the saffron with butter and dot over the surface of the pulao.

Cabbage and Carrot Pulao
(Gobi Aur Gajar Ka Pulao)

This is a very colourful dish with its orange flecks of carrot. In India there is even a variety of carrot, available in winter, which is such a deep, deep orange it is almost red. They are particularly delicious when used to make halvas (see recipes on page 120) – and very beautiful. I have never seen these red carrots outside the sub-continent, but you will find that this pulao is just as colourful with ordinary carrots.

500 G (1 LB) BASMATI RICE

3 TABLESPOONS GHEE

2 ONIONS, SLICED

1 TEASPOON BLACK CUMIN SEEDS

4–6 GREEN CARDAMOMS

1 X 5 CM (2 INCH) PIECE CINNAMON STICK, HALVED

6 BLACK PEPPERCORNS

1 X 5 CM (2 INCH) PIECE FRESH GINGER, SHREDDED

1½ TEASPOONS SALT

½ SMALL WHITE CABBAGE, GRATED

3 CARROTS, GRATED

900 ML (1½ PINTS) WATER

Wash the rice thoroughly and set aside in a strainer to drain.

Melt the ghee in a heavy-based saucepan, add the onions, black cumin seeds, green cardamoms, cinnamon, peppercorns, shredded ginger and salt and fry until some bits are darker than others.

Using a slotted spoon, stir the rice in, followed by the grated cabbage and half the grated carrot.

Continue to stir-fry for about 3 minutes, then pour in the water, bring to the boil, lower the heat to medium, cover the pan and cook for 15–20 minutes, until the rice is tender and the water has been absorbed.

Before serving the rice, stir in the remaining carrots.

Panir Pulao

Panir, also known as 'paneer' is an important ingredient in Indian vegetarian cooking. You will find it in specialist Asian grocers and delicatessens. If you have difficulty in obtaining it, you will find a recipe for making your own in the chapter on curries, on page 74. It is a very versatile ingredient – you can dice it and fry it until golden, as in this recipe, or crumble it so that it looks a little like ricotta or cottage cheese. I prefer it fried, as in this recipe, and it is easily adapted to other vegetable recipes if you would like to raise the protein content of a particular menu.

2 TABLESPOONS GHEE

¼ TEASPOON ONION SEEDS

¼ TEASPOON MUSTARD SEEDS

4 DRIED RED CHILLIES

¼ TEASPOON WHITE CUMIN SEEDS

4 CURRY LEAVES

1 ONION, SLICED

2 TOMATOES, SLICED

1 TABLESPOON FRESH CORIANDER

2 GREEN CHILLIES

1 TEASPOON SALT

2 CUPS RICE

3 CUPS WATER

6 TABLESPOONS OIL

250 G (8 OZ) PANIR, CUT

IN 2.5 CM (1 INCH) CUBES

Heat the ghee in a heavy-based saucepan over a medium heat, add the onion seeds, mustard seeds, dried red chillies, cumin seeds and curry leaves and fry for about 1 minute. Add the onion and fry until golden brown.

Stir in the tomatoes, fresh coriander, green chillies, salt and rice and stir-fry for 1 minute. using a slotted spoon. Pour in the water and bring to the boil, lower the heat, cover the pan and cook for 15–20 minutes, or until the rice is tender and the water has been absorbed.

Meanwhile, heat the oil in a frying pan, add the panir cubes and fry them until lightly browned. Remove the cubes from the pan with a slotted spoon and set aside on absorbent kitchen paper to drain.

When the rice is cooked, turn it out on to a serving dish and decorate with the panir cubes before serving.

Peas and Panir Pulao
(Matar Panir Pulao)

This pulao makes a delicious and impressive centrepiece for a special occasion meal. It is excellent served with Masala Sweetcorn Raita (see page 108).

250 G (8 OZ) NATURAL YOGURT

100 ML (4 FL OZ) SINGLE CREAM

1½ TEASPOONS GARAM MASALA

1 TEASPOON GARLIC PULP

¼ TEASPOON TURMERIC

1 TEASPOON CHILLI POWDER

½ TEASPOON BLACK CUMIN SEEDS

½ TEASPOON CARDAMOM SEEDS, CRUSHED

1 TEASPOON GINGER PULP

1½ TEASPOONS SALT

6 TABLESPOONS PURE GHEE OR BUTTER

3 CLOVES

2 BAY LEAVES

2 ONIONS, SLICED

2 TABLESPOONS TOMATO PURÉE

175 G (6 OZ) PEAS

2 TABLESPOONS CHOPPED FRESH CORIANDER

3 TABLESPOONS LEMON JUICE

250 G (8 OZ) PANIR, CUT IN 2.5 CM (1 INCH) CUBES

2 CUPS RICE

900 ML (1½ PINTS) WATER

1 TEASPOON SAFFRON STRANDS, CRUSHED

2 TOMATOES, SLICED

2 GREEN CHILLIES, CHOPPED

Whisk the yogurt and cream together and add the garam masala, garlic, turmeric, chilli powder, black cumin seeds, crushed cardamom seeds, ginger and salt. Mix thoroughly and set aside.

Heat the ghee or butter in a saucepan, add the cloves, bay leaves and onions. Fry for 3 minutes, then lower the heat and add the tomato purée, peas, fresh coriander and lemon juice.

Next pour in the yogurt and spice mixture and cook, stirring occasionally, for 5–7 minutes. When the sauce has thickened, add the panir cubes, remove from the heat and set aside.

Wash the rice and tip it into a saucepan of lightly salted boiling water. Add the saffron strands. Partly cook the rice (so that it still has a 'bone in the middle'). Drain the part-cooked rice into a strainer and set aside.

Line the bottom of a deep ovenproof dish with the sliced tomato and green chillies and pour the panir sauce in. Pour the rice on top of this and cover the dish with a tight-fitting lid or with foil and cook in a preheated moderate oven, 180°C (350°F), Gas Mark 4 for 15–20 minutes.

Remove from the oven and leave to stand for 5–7 minutes before removing the cover and turning out on a serving dish.

Breads

No Indian meal, especially in the north, is
complete without bread. There are many kinds
in India, most of them unleavened, that is,
without yeast. The most popular in the West is
the leavened bread, naan (see page 34). This
chapter includes a selection of unleavened
breads, including chapatis and paratas.

Chapati

Chapatis are probably the best known of the Indian unleavened breads in the West. They are always circular, and measure about 15–17 cm (6–7 inches) in diameter. No fat is used in making the bread, which is cooked on a thawa, a cast-iron flat pan or griddle with a handle, available from Indian or Pakistani stores. It is best to use a cloth, rolled up into a round shape, to move the chapati around on the thawa. In India chapatis are cooked on a naked flame so that they puff up. Allow about 2 per person.

425 G (14 OZ) ATA (CHAPATI FLOUR)
1 TEASPOON SALT
300 ML (½ PINT) WATER

Sift the flour into a deep bowl. Make a well in the centre, add the salt and water, and mix together to form a soft dough.

Gather the dough from the sides of the bowl and knead with the back of your fist until the dough is pliable. Cover and leave to stand for about 10 minutes. Divide into 8 pieces and roll each one into a ball between the palms of your hands. Dust them with flour to prevent the dough sticking, and roll out to form a circle approximately 15 cm (6 inches) in diameter.

Heat the thawa to a very high temperature and add a chapati. After about 10–15 seconds, turn it over, pressing down with the cloth and moving the chapati around the thawa. Turn it over again and repeat, moving the chapati around. Make sure it is cooked, especially around the edges, then remove from the thawa. Repeat with the other chapatis.

Like all Indian breads, chapatis are best served as soon as possible after making. As they are cooked, keep them warm, covered in foil, piled on top of each other. Brush each one with a little butter if desired, to help keep it moist.

Masala Puri

Puris are best fried in a karahi and eaten straight away, usually with a curry. They may also be made with ordinary wholemeal flour instead of the traditional 'ata', or chapati flour.

250 G (8 OZ) ATA (CHAPATI FLOUR)
1 TEASPOON SALT
½ TEASPOON ONION SEEDS
½ TEASPOON CRUSHED DRIED RED CHILLIES
1 GREEN CHILLI, DICED
1 TABLESPOON CHOPPED FRESH CORIANDER
½ TEASPOON BICARBONATE OF SODA
175 ML (6 FL OZ) WATER
OIL FOR FRYING (SEE METHOD)

Sift the flour and salt into a deep bowl and make a well in the centre. Mix in the onion seeds, the red and green chillies, coriander and bicarbonate of soda.

Gradually pour in sufficient water and, using your fingertips, mix to form a soft dough. Wipe the bowl clean with the ball of dough. Using the back of your hand, knead the dough for about 1 minute and leave to stand for 5–7 minutes.

Heat the oil, preferably in a karahi. Break small balls off the dough about the size of a golf ball and roll out on a lightly floured surface into 10–12 cm (4–5 inch) circular shapes.

Drop each puri into the hot oil, pressing down gently with a slotted spoon so that the puri is fully covered with oil. Gently turn it over, fry for a further 30 seconds, then remove. Drain off as much oil as possible back into the karahi and place the puri on a tray lined with kitchen paper to absorb any more oil.

Serve the puris immediately, allowing 2–3 per person.

Puri

250 G (8 OZ) ATA (CHAPATI FLOUR)
½ TEASPOON SALT
1 TABLESPOON OIL
½ TEASPOON BICARBONATE OF SODA
100–125 ML (3½–4 FL OZ) WATER
300 ML (½ PINT) CORN OIL
50 G (2 OZ) FLOUR, FOR DUSTING

Sift the flour into a deep bowl. Make a well in the centre and add the salt, oil and bicarbonate of soda. Stir in the measured water and, using your fingertips, gather in all the flour to form a soft pliable dough. Set aside.

Heat the oil in a karahi or deep frying pan. Once the oil is hot, reduce the heat to medium. Break off small balls of dough, making about 12, and roll out on a lightly floured surface to 15 cm (6 inch) diameter rounds. Deep-fry the puris one by one, turning each at least once. Serve immediately.

PREVIOUS PAGES: *A selection of Indian breads, which are always best served hot, immediately after making. Clockwise from bottom left are Potato Roti – Aloo Ki Roti – (recipe page 103), Chapati (recipe above) and Stuffed Paratas (recipe page 103).*
ILLUSTRATED ON FRONTISPIECE: *Indian breads, including Besun Ki Roti (recipe page 103) and Chapatis.*

Stuffed Paratas

2 POTATOES, SLICED
1½ TEASPOONS SALT
2 GREEN CHILLIES, CHOPPED
½ TEASPOON CRUSHED RED CHILLIES
1 TEASPOON CHILLI POWDER
2 TEASPOONS MANGO POWDER
1 TABLESPOON CHOPPED FRESH CORIANDER
2 TABLESPOONS FLOUR, FOR DUSTING
4–6 TABLESPOONS MELTED GHEE
PARATA DOUGH
375 G (12 OZ) CHAPATI FLOUR
1 TEASPOON SALT
WATER TO FORM A SOFT DOUGH (SEE METHOD)

Boil the potatoes until soft. Drain, then mash with the salt, chillies, chilli powder, mango powder and coriander. Set aside.

To make the dough, sift the flour and salt into a bowl, make a well in the centre. Gradually add water, mixing it in with your fingers, to make a soft dough. Knead it on a flat surface, using your knuckles. Leave to stand for 10–15 minutes.

Break off balls slightly smaller than a tennis ball and make them into flat, round shapes, using the palm of your hand. On a lightly floured surface, roll the shapes out to about 15 cm (6 inches). Put about a tablespoonful of the potato mixture into each parata and bring the edges together into the middle to make a round ball. Gently flatten it, then roll out to about a 25 cm (10 inch) round. Dust the parata with flour, if necessary.

Heat a thawa or flat griddle until it begins to steam. Gently lift each parata on to the thawa, pouring 1 teaspoon of ghee on top. With a flat spoon or a spatula, turn each parata over and fry it, slowly moving it about. Pour over another teaspoon of ghee and turn over again. Fry for a further 30 seconds, remove and serve with mango chutney, if liked.

Paratas

300 G (10 OZ) ATA (CHAPATI FLOUR)
1 TEASPOON SALT
150 ML (¼ PINT) WATER
FLOUR FOR DUSTING
3 TABLESPOONS GHEE

Make the dough as above, divide into 6–8 portions and roll out on a floured surface. Brush the middle with ½ teaspoon ghee. Fold the dough in half and roll up into a tube. Flatten it with your palms, then coil round your fingers. Roll out to about 18 cm (7 inch) diameter, dusting with flour as necessary.

Heat a thawa or heavy-based frying-pan and slap a parata on to it (paratas should be cooked one at a time). Cook as in the previous recipe, moving, turning and brushing with ghee. Remove and keep warm until ready to serve.

Besun Ki Roti

Made with both ata (chapati flour) and gram flour (besun), then flavoured with chilli and coriander, this roti is delicious with any of the curries in this book. Serve 2 per person.

125 G (4 OZ) ATA (CHAPATI FLOUR)
75 G (3 OZ) GRAM FLOUR (BESUN)
½ TEASPOON SALT
1 TEASPOON CRUSHED DRIED RED CHILLIES
2 RED CHILLIES, FINELY CHOPPED
1 SMALL ONION, FINELY DICED
1 TABLESPOON CHOPPED FRESH CORIANDER
1 TEASPOON CHOPPED FRESH MINT
150 ML (¼ PINT) WATER
2 TABLESPOONS GHEE

Sift the two flours and salt into a large bowl. With your fingers, mix in the dried and fresh chillies, onion, coriander and mint.

Gradually stir in the water, form it into a soft dough and knead for about 5 minutes. Divide the dough into 8 portions. Roll out each portion of dough on a lightly floured surface to about 18 cm (7 inches) diameter.

Heat a thawa or heavy-based frying pan. Pick each roti up gently and place it on to the thawa. Grease the top with about ½ teaspoon ghee and cook, turning it over 2–3 times or until you are sure the roti is cooked. Serve hot.

Potato Roti
(Aloo Ki Roti)

3 POTATOES, PEELED
1 TEASPOON CRUSHED DRIED RED CHILLIES
2 GREEN CHILLIES, CHOPPED
1 TABLESPOON CHOPPED FRESH CORIANDER
1½ TEASPOONS MANGO POWDER
1 TEASPOON SALT
2 TABLESPOONS UNSALTED BUTTER, MELTED
150 G (5 OZ) PLAIN FLOUR
CORN OIL FOR FRYING
FLOUR FOR DUSTING

Boil the potatoes, drain and mash. Mix in the dried and fresh chillies, coriander, mango powder, salt and butter.

Gradually stir in the flour to form a soft dough. Divide into 6 pieces, then roll out to 12 cm (5 inch) rounds. Set aside.

Heat a thawa or a griddle, gently place a roti on to the thawa, drop about 1 teaspoon of oil around the edges and lift them gently so the oil slips under the roti. Pour another teaspoon of oil on top of the roti and gently turn it over.

When lightly browned, remove and set aside. Cook all the rotis in the same way and serve hot with curry or a dhaal.

Accompaniments

Mouth-watering side dishes are a traditional
part of almost every Indian meal, including
breakfast. Try raitas – cooling or spicy – and
chutneys, pickles, relishes or kachumbers, as
well as some unusual salads and sauces.

Apple Chutney
(Seb Ki Chutney)

No Indian meal is complete without a chutney or relish – and they suit many Western meals as well. They can be sweet or sour, or both at the same time. They can also be spicy or mild. They can be freshly made to eat immediately, or bottled for future use, the way jams and pickles are in European cookery. There are many good ones available in shops and supermarkets, but I think there's nothing to beat the ones you make yourself.

Apples do not flourish in tropical climates, so the best apples in India come from the state of Kashmir, which also produces wonderful apple juice. Apple chutney is well-known in Britain, where it was introduced by people who had come to appreciate chutneys while working for the East India Company or the military or Civil Service when India became part of the British Empire. This one may be served as an accompaniment to any of the curries in this book.

1 KG (2 LB) GREEN APPLES
150 ML (¼ PINT) WATER
175 G (6 OZ) BROWN SUGAR
½ TEASPOON GARAM MASALA
1 TEASPOON CHILLI POWDER
1 TEASPOON GARLIC PULP
300 ML (½ PINT) MALT VINEGAR
1 TEASPOON SALT
1 TEASPOON CHOPPED FRESH MINT

Peel and dice the apples roughly. Place them in a medium saucepan and add the measured water.

In a small bowl, mix the brown sugar, garam masala, chilli powder, garlic, malt vinegar and salt together. Pour the mixture into the saucepan and cook over a medium heat, mashing down the apples occasionally, leaving some pieces whole so that the apples are not completely mashed.

Once all the liquid is evaporated, add the chopped mint and mix in well.

Transfer the chutney to a bowl to cool. Once it has cooled, transfer it to a clean dry jar, cover and refrigerate. It will keep for 2–3 days.

PREVIOUS PAGES: *From left, Plum Chutney (recipe page 107), Date and Tamarind Chutney (recipe page 110) and Apple Chutney (recipe above). Chutneys were enthusiastically adopted by the British under the Raj, who took them back to England where they are now found in almost every store cupboard – the perfect way to enliven sandwiches and cold dishes. They can be made more or less hot by varying the chilli content.*

Hot Mint and Coriander Chutney
(Mirch, Podinay Aur Haray Dhania Ki Chutney)

This might be called a 'fresh' chutney, since it is made just before serving. It is very good with samosas and pakoras and a dish of it on the table will perk up even the simplest meal. It is best made in a food processor, as the ingredients need to be blended well together. If you do not have one, then just chop the fresh ingredients as finely as possible.

3 TABLESPOONS CHOPPED FRESH MINT
3 TABLESPOONS CHOPPED FRESH CORIANDER
2 GREEN CHILLIES, FINELY CHOPPED
1 TEASPOON GARAM MASALA
½ TEASPOON CHILLI POWDER
1 TEASPOON SUGAR
1 LEVEL TEASPOON SALT
2 TABLESPOONS LEMON JUICE

Mix all the ingredients, except the lemon juice, together with a fork, or put them in a food processor and blend until smooth.

Tip the chutney into a bowl, stir in the lemon juice and serve.

Green Tomato Chutney

If you grow your own tomatoes, this recipe is perfect for using up end-of-season fruit which hasn't ripened properly.

1 KG (2 LB) GREEN TOMATOES, ROUGHLY CHOPPED
2 SMALL ONIONS, ROUGHLY CHOPPED
2 GREEN CHILLIES, FINELY CHOPPED
½ TEASPOON GINGER PULP
3 TABLESPOONS CHOPPED FRESH CORIANDER
1 LEVEL TEASPOON SALT
2 TABLESPOONS LEMON JUICE

Place the tomatoes and onions in a food processor. Add the green chillies, ginger and coriander and blend coarsely.

Spoon the chutney into a bowl and add lemon juice to taste. Chill until ready to serve.

VARIATION
Green Mango Chutney
Substitute a similar quantity of green mango flesh – you will need more than 1 kg (2 lb) because much of the weight of a mango is in the seed.

Coconut Chutney

This is another 'fresh' chutney, which should be served as soon as it is ready. It is quite popular in the south of India, where coconuts are widely grown, and is usually served with dosai (recipe on page 22). Though it is nice to use freshly grated coconut for this chutney, ordinary desiccated coconut is just as good.

2 TABLESPOONS CHANA DHAAL
175 G (6 OZ) DESICCATED COCONUT
½ TEASPOON GARLIC PULP
½ TEASPOON GINGER PULP
½ TEASPOON CRUSHED DRIED RED CHILLIES
1 TEASPOON SALT
2 GREEN CHILLIES, CHOPPED
1 TABLESPOON FRESH CORIANDER
3 TABLESPOONS LEMON JUICE
2 TABLESPOONS CORN OIL
4–6 CURRY LEAVES
½ TEASPOONS MUSTARD SEEDS
125 G (4 OZ) NATURAL YOGURT

Boil the chana dhaal in water to cover until soft enough to be mashed. Mash the dhaal with a wooden masher and set aside.

Put the coconut, garlic, ginger, crushed red chillies, salt, green chillies, fresh coriander and lemon juice in a food processor or blender and grind for about 30 seconds. Add the mixture to the chana dhaal.

Heat the oil in a small frying pan, add the curry leaves and mustard seeds and fry for a minute or so, until they are a shade darker. Pour the hot oil with the seeds and leaves on to the coconut mixture. Stir in the yogurt and serve.

Plum Chutney

This is probably one of my favourite accompaniments. It is very versatile and, with its distinct sweet-and-sour flavour, goes well with almost any vegetarian Indian dish.

1 KG (2 LB) RED PLUMS
1 TEASPOON GINGER PULP
1 TEASPOON CHILLI POWDER
2 TEASPOONS MANGO POWDER
1 TEASPOON GROUND CORIANDER
1 TEASPOON GROUND CUMIN
250 G (8 OZ) BROWN SUGAR
1 TEASPOON SALT
300 ML (½ PINT) MALT VINEGAR
150 ML (¼ PINT) WATER
75 G (3 OZ) SULTANAS

Cut the plums in half, remove and discard the stones. Chop the fruit roughly and place them in a medium-sized saucepan.

Blend together the ginger, chilli powder, mango powder, ground coriander, cumin, brown sugar, salt, malt vinegar and water together. Pour the mixture over the plums in the saucepan and bring to the boil.

Reduce the heat, add the sultanas and cook, uncovered, until the plums are soft and all the liquid has been absorbed.

Transfer the chutney to a bowl and allow it to cool. The plum chutney will keep for up to 4 weeks stored in covered jars in the refrigerator.

Mango Chutney

A wonderful way to serve India's favourite fruit. This version uses sweet, ripe mangoes. If you have green mangoes, follow the recipe for Green Tomato Chutney (page 106), rather than this one, substituting green mangoes for green tomatoes.

3 LARGE, RIPE MANGOES, PEELED AND SLICED
½ TEASPOON ASAFOETIDA POWDER (OPTIONAL)
2.5 CM (1 INCH) FRESH ROOT GINGER, GRATED
1 TEASPOON CHILLI POWDER
2 TEASPOONS MANGO POWDER
1 TABLESPOON CHOPPED FRESH MINT LEAVES
1 TEASPOON GROUND CUMIN
1 TABLESPOON BROWN SUGAR
1 TEASPOON SALT
LEMON JUICE (OPTIONAL)

Place all the ingredients in a food processor and blend briefly until mixed. Spoon into a serving dish, adding a little lemon juice if the mixture is too thick.

Aubergine Raita

Although raitas can be very cooling dishes to serve with spicy food, this one isn't, thanks to the fresh green chillies and dried red ones. To cool your palate, I include a recipe for a cool Cucumber Raita below, right.

1 AUBERGINE, DICED

1 ONION, DICED

2 TABLESPOONS CORN OIL

½ TEASPOON ONION SEEDS

4 CURRY LEAVES

3 DRIED RED CHILLIES

2 GARLIC CLOVES

2 TOMATOES, DICED

2 GREEN CHILLIES, CHOPPED

1 TABLESPOON CHOPPED FRESH CORIANDER

1 TABLESPOON CHOPPED FRESH MINT LEAVES

175 G (6 OZ) NATURAL YOGURT

75 G (3 OZ) WATER

1 TEASPOON SALT

2 MINT SPRIGS, TO GARNISH

Set the prepared aubergine and onion dice to one side.

Heat the oil in a medium-sized saucepan and fry the onion seeds for about 30 seconds before adding the curry leaves, dried red chillies and garlic cloves. Fry these for another minute, lowering the heat, if necessary.

Add the aubergine, onion and tomatoes to the saucepan and continue frying for about 5 minutes, stirring occasionally.

Gradually add the green chillies, fresh coriander and mint and stir to mix. Remove from the heat and set aside.

In a serving dish, whisk the natural yogurt along with the water and salt.

Pour the aubergine mixture over the top of the yogurt and gently mix together.

Serve garnished with the mint sprigs.

Masala Sweetcorn Raita

Raitas are among the most versatile of all accompaniments. They can be served with almost any curry or meal. There are several ways raitas can be made, using ingredients such as cucumber, tomato, aubergines and onions.

2 TABLESPOONS CORN OIL

¼ TEASPOON ONION SEEDS

4 DRIED RED CHILLIES, WHOLE

1 SMALL ONION, CHOPPED

250 G (8 OZ) SWEETCORN KERNELS, CANNED OR FROZEN

1 TEASPOON CHILLI POWDER

½ TEASPOON GROUND CORIANDER

1 TEASPOON SALT

2 TABLESPOONS CHOPPED FRESH CORIANDER

300 G (10 OZ) NATURAL YOGURT

6 CHERRY TOMATOES

SPRIG OF MINT

Heat the oil in a heavy-based saucepan over a medium heat and fry the onion seeds, chillies and onion for about 1 minute. Add the sweetcorn, then the chilli powder, ground coriander and salt. Fry for about 2 minutes, stirring occasionally. Once all the liquid has been absorbed by the sweetcorn mixture, set the corn aside to cool for about 10 minutes.

Meanwhile, mix the fresh coriander with the yogurt and set aside in a serving dish.

Pour the cooled sweetcorn into the yogurt and decorate with the cherry tomatoes and the mint sprig.

Cucumber Raita

This is the raita to cool the fires if you have been too enthusiastic with the chillies in other dishes. Try to find small cucumbers so that your raita will look more attractive. Yogurt is also very good for people with upset tummies.

300 G (10 OZ) NATURAL YOGURT

1 CUCUMBER, SLICED, SALTED AND DRAINED

½ TEASPOON GROUND CUMIN

½ TEASPOON SALT

1 TEASPOON SUGAR

1 TEASPOON LEMON JUICE (OPTIONAL)

Whip the yogurt, stir in the cumin, salt and sugar, add the cucumber, taste and add lemon juice, if liked. Refrigerate the raita for at least 1 hour before serving.

RIGHT: *From top, Masala Sweetcorn Raita (recipe above, right) and Aubergine Raita (recipe above). Though raitas are often used as a cooling contrast to spicy curries, these two aren't – they are wonderfully spicy in their own right. If you would like a more cooling effect, try the Cucumber Raita (recipe right).*

Tamarind and Sesame Seed Chutney
(Imli Aur Thill Ki Chutney)

Tamarind, or 'imli', is a very popular flavouring in India – a little tart, like lime or lemon juice. This is a very typical Hyderabadi chutney. It makes a delicious accompaniment to a wide variety of dishes. It also makes a good base for salad sandwiches.

125 G (4 OZ) RED TAMARIND BLOCK
175 ML (6 OZ) HOT WATER
1 TEASPOON SUGAR
300 G (10 OZ) SESAME SEEDS
2 GREEN CHILLIES, CHOPPED
2 TABLESPOONS CHOPPED FRESH CORIANDER
1 TEASPOON SALT
1 ONION, DICED
SPRIG OF FRESH CORIANDER

Place the tamarind block in the hot water and leave for about 15 minutes. Squeeze the pulp out and push through a sieve into a bowl to give a purée.

Add the sugar and set aside.

Dry roast the sesame seeds in a small saucepan until they change colour a little. Once they are cool, put them in a food processor and grind until powdery. Add the chillies, chopped coriander, salt and half the onion and blend together.

Stir the blended spices into the tamarind pulp, adding a little water, if necessary, to loosen the mixture.

Pour the chutney into a serving dish and serve garnished with the remaining onions and the coriander.

Date and Tamarind Chutney

This chutney has a delicious and mouth-watering sweet-and-sour flavour, provided by the sweet dates and lemony tamarind. Serve it with any of the snacks or starters or as an accompaniment to any meal.

25G (1 OZ) SULTANAS
250 G (8 OZ) PITTED DATES
150 ML (¼ PINT) HOT WATER
1 TABLESPOON RED TAMARIND PASTE
2 TABLESPOONS BROWN SUGAR
1 TEASPOON CHILLI POWDER
2 TEASPOONS GROUND CORIANDER
1 TEASPOON GROUND CUMIN
1 TEASPOON SALT
1 TEASPOON GINGER POWDER
3 TABLESPOONS BROWN MALT VINEGAR

Rinse the sultanas and dates, drain and place in a saucepan with the hot water. Bring to the boil. Remove the pan from the heat and add the tamarind, brown sugar, chilli powder, ground coriander, ground cumin, salt, ginger powder and malt vinegar.

Return to the heat and cook for about 1–2 minutes. Remove from the heat and leave to cool for about 10 minutes.

Place in a food processor and grind for about 30 seconds.

Transfer the chutney to a serving dish or jars. The chutney will keep in jars for about a week.

VARIATION
Tamarind Chutney with Apricots, Apples or Peaches
This chutney may also be made substituting 250 g (8 oz) of apricots or peaches, stoned, peeled and cut into chunks, or a similar quantity of apples, which have been peeled, cored and quartered. Choose very ripe, fresh apricots, or the yellow variety of peaches, very ripe and soft. Apricots are native to China, but spread west to India, and then into Europe, brought back by the returning armies of Alexander the Great. Apricots grow now in Kashmir, as do so many temperate zone fruits.

Illustrated on page 104.

Vadde

Vadde deep-fried dumplings are very popular in the north-western state of Gujarat. They are wonderfully crunchy, spicy and very easy to make. Serve them either hot or cold. They are delicious as a starter, and equally good with other dishes. Always serve a dipping sauce or chutney with them.

250 ML (8 OZ) URID DHAAL
½ BUNCH SPRING ONIONS, FINELY CHOPPED
1½ TEASPOONS CRUSHED CORIANDER
1 TEASPOON GINGER PULP
1 TEASPOON FENNEL SEEDS
½ TEASPOON BICARBONATE OF SODA
1 TEASPOON SALT
4 GREEN CHILLIES, CHOPPED
2 TABLESPOONS FRESH CORIANDER
CORN OIL FOR FRYING (SEE METHOD)
125 G (4 OZ) COARSE SEMOLINA

Soak the urid dhaal for several hours, preferably overnight. Drain thoroughly and blend to a purée in a food processor. Transfer the urid dhaal purée to a medium-size bowl.

Add the spring onions, crushed coriander, ginger pulp, fennel seeds, bicarbonate of soda, salt, green chillies and fresh coriander to the urid dhaal purée and mix together.

Press small balls of the mixture into rounds in the palms of your hands and make a hole in the middle of each one.

Heat the oil in a frying pan, dip each vada into the semolina, and fry them in the hot oil, turning at least twice and gently pressing them down with the back of a spoon.

Once all the vadde are fried, serve them hot with Spicy Tomato Ketchup (recipe page 117).

Tomato and Onion Salad

This combination is as popular in India as it is in the West – so common that you might overlook it as an accompaniment for a special occasion dinner party. Don't – it's very good!

4 RIPE TOMATOES
1 ONION, FINELY SLICED
1 TABLESPOON CHOPPED FRESH CORIANDER
1 LEMON, CUT INTO WEDGES, TO GARNISH (OPTIONAL)

Place the tomatoes in a serving dish and scatter over the onion and coriander. Garnish with lemon wedges if liked.

VARIATION
Tomato and Onion Salad with Carrot and Lettuce
Add 2–3 lettuce leaves, finely shredded and 1 carrot, grated or sliced, to the main recipe.

Banana and Coconut Salad

This salad couldn't be simpler – and is a very cooling accompaniment for a fiery curry. Never drink water if you find your curry was too spicy – it won't do any good at all. Instead, eat yogurt or a banana. Never keep bananas in the refrigerator – they don't like it. And don't keep them in the same fruit bowl as citrus fruit, because they will ripen and go soft much too quickly.

2 LARGE RIPE BANANAS
1 TABLESPOON LEMON JUICE
1 TABLESPOON DESICCATED COCONUT

Peel and slice the bananas into an attractive serving bowl. Brush with the lemon juice to prevent the bananas from browning, then sprinkle over the coconut.

Mooli and Carrot Salad
(Mooli Aurgajar Ki Salad)

Mooli, also known as Japanese radish, or 'daikon', is from the same family as ordinary red garden radishes, and is now widely available from most supermarkets and grocers. It is long, like a cucumber, white and usually sold by weight. It has a lovely crunchy flavour – milder than the red variety – and goes particularly well with carrots.

1 MOOLI, ABOUT 15–20 CM (6–8 INCHES), PEELED
2 CARROTS (ABOUT SAME WEIGHT AS MOOLI)
½ CUCUMBER
2 TABLESPOONS LIME JUICE
1 TABLESPOON HONEY
1 TEASPOON SALT
1 TEASPOON CHOPPED FRESH CORIANDER
1 TABLESPOON CHOPPED FRESH MINT
½ TEASPOON CRUSHED DRIED RED CHILLIES
2 RED CHILLIES, SLICED

Using the blade that grates very finely in your food processor, grate the mooli and the carrots. Mix together and set aside. Wash and cut the cucumber into very thin 5 cm (2 inch) chips.

Place the grated mooli, carrots and cucumber chips in an attractive serving dish.

In a separate bowl, mix the lime juice, honey, salt, coriander, mint and crushed red chillies together. Pour this mixture over the vegetables and serve garnished with sliced red chillies.

Fruit and Vegetable Salad

This is not exactly a typical Indian salad, but it may be a variation on a coleslaw. Do try it any time of the day, or as a starter.

8–10 BLACK GRAPES, HALVED AND DESEEDED
8–10 WHITE GRAPES, HALVED AND DESEEDED
2 BANANAS, SLICED
2 RED APPLES, DICED
½ CUCUMBER, SLICED
1 LARGE CARROT, SLICED
4 ICEBERG LETTUCE LEAVES, CHOPPED
250 G (8 OZ) GREEK YOGURT
1 TEASPOON SUGAR
1 TEASPOON SALT
½ TEASPOON CHILLI POWDER
½ TEASPOON GROUND CORIANDER
1 TABLESPOON CHOPPED FRESH MINT
25 G (1 OZ) WALNUTS, HALVED
SPRIG OF MINT

Place the prepared fruit and vegetables in a glass bowl.

Mix together the yogurt, sugar, salt, chilli powder, ground coriander and chopped mint. Pour the yogurt mixture over the salad and mix in gently.

Garnish the salad with the walnuts and the sprig of mint and serve chilled.

VARIATION

Banana, Coconut and Lemon Salad

There are many delicious varieties of bananas in India, ranging from very small and sweet yellow ones to large red ones.

However the ordinary large ones imported from the Caribbean, sometimes known as 'Cavendish' bananas, are perfect in this salad. Instead of the grapes and apples in the main recipe, substitute 2 ripe bananas, 1 tablespoon sweet desiccated coconut and 1 tablespoon lemon juice. Proceed as in the main recipe.

Grated Mooli Salad

Mooli – also known as 'daikon' or Japanese radish – is widely available in Asian greengrocers, and bigger supermarkets. It is often eaten sliced on its own as a salad accompaniment. In this recipe the mooli is grated and served in a yogurt sauce garnished with seasoned oil.

750 G (1½ LB) MOOLI, GRATED
300 G (10 OZ) NATURAL YOGURT
1 TEASPOON SUGAR
1 TEASPOON SALT
1 TABLESPOON FRESH CORIANDER
1 TABLESPOON FRESH MINT
2 FRESH RED CHILLIES, CHOPPED
150 ML (¼ PINT) WATER
1 TABLESPOON OIL
¼ TEASPOON MUSTARD SEEDS
4 CURRY LEAVES
TO GARNISH
PINCH OF GROUND CUMIN
PINCH OF GROUND CORIANDER
PINCH OF CHILLI POWDER

Set the grated mooli aside in a serving dish.

Whisk together the yogurt, sugar, salt, coriander, mint, chopped chillies and water and pour over the mooli.

Heat the oil in a small pan and fry the mustard seeds and curry leaves in the hot oil until they turn a shade darker. Pour the oil (and the seeds and curry leaves) on the yogurt while still hot. Sprinkle over the cumin powder, coriander powder and chilli powder.

VARIATION

Mooli Salad with Coconut and a Spicy Dressing

Add 1 tablespoon desiccated coconut to the above recipe. Mix 150 ml (¼ pint) corn oil with 1 tablespoon onion seeds and ¼ teaspoon crushed dried red chillies, then spoon over the salad. Keep any surplus oil dressing in a screwtop jar in the refrigerator.

LEFT: *From top, Fruit and Vegetable Salad (recipe above) and Grated Mooli Salad (recipe above, right). Salads are as important in Indian cooking as in Western cuisine, providing a delicious contrast in flavour and texture. Both these recipes can be varied according to which fruits and vegetables are in season.*

Sweet and Sour Tomato and Onion Relish

This is a very versatile and delicious accompaniment.

2 TABLESPOONS CORN OIL

2 TEASPOONS BROWN SUGAR

2 GARLIC CLOVES, HALVED

1 ONION, CHOPPED

SALT TO TASTE

¼ TEASPOON CRUSHED DRIED RED CHILLIES

1 FRESH GREEN CHILLI, CHOPPED

3 TABLESPOONS MALT VINEGAR

2 TOMATOES, DESEEDED AND SLICED

1 GREEN PEPPER, DESEEDED AND SLICED

1 TABLESPOON CHOPPED FRESH CORIANDER

Heat the oil in a deep frying pan over a medium heat, lower the heat and sprinkle in the brown sugar. Fry it lightly.

Add the garlic cloves, followed by the onion. Continue frying for about 2 minutes. Add the salt, crushed red chillies and green chilli and stir-fry.

Reduce the heat and pour the malt vinegar into the pan, then add the tomatoes, green pepper and fresh coriander and continue to stir-fry for a further 3–5 minutes.

Transfer the relish to an attractive serving dish. It may be served hot or cold.

RIGHT: *From top, Onion and Cucumber Relish (recipe right) and Sweet and Sour Tomato and Onion Relish (recipe above). Relishes, like chutneys, were 'borrowed' from India and adapted to British cooking by people who had worked for the British East India Company, or later for the military or civil service when India became part of the Empire. Englishmen developed a taste for spice and curry, and these delicious concoctions seemed to add flavour and interest to the bland foods of their native England. In India, relishes are used as a contrast to more substantial dishes, such as curries.*

Onion Relish

Use small onions for this relish as they make a better-looking salad when the onions are cut into rings. There are many varieties in India, ranging from the shallot types in the south, to the small round red ones in the north. Onions are served with most meals in Indian households except in the prosperous, vegetarian Jain community, who eat no root vegetables of any kind.

2 TABLESPOONS CHOPPED FRESH MINT

2 TABLESPOONS CHOPPED FRESH CORIANDER

1 GREEN CHILLI, CHOPPED

1 RED CHILLI, CHOPPED

½ TEASPOON SALT

4 SMALL ONIONS

1 LIME

½ TEASPOON BLACK PEPPERCORNS, CRUSHED

Mix the chopped mint, coriander, green and red chillies and salt together in a bowl.

Peel the onions, cut in rings and place on a serving dish.

Cut the lime in four quarters and squeeze the juice from two of them on to the onions. Stir the mint mixture into the onions and sprinkle the crushed black peppercorns over the top.

Garnish with the remaining lime quarters.

Onion and Cucumber Relish

Relishes are an important part of any meal as they not only help to perk it up but also help turn an ordinary meal into an interesting one.

1 LARGE BUNCH SPRING ONIONS, FINELY CHOPPED

1 ONION, FINELY DICED

1 CUCUMBER, FINELY DICED

1 TABLESPOON CHOPPED FRESH MINT

1 TABLESPOON CHOPPED FRESH CORIANDER

2 TABLESPOONS LEMON JUICE

½ TEASPOON SALT

2 RED CHILLIES

CRUSHED BLACK PEPPERCORNS

TO GARNISH

SPRIG OF CORIANDER

SPRIG OF MINT

Mix the spring onions, onion, cucumber, mint and coriander together. Add the lemon juice and salt and mix thoroughly.

Mix in the red chillies and sprinkle on the black pepper. Serve the dish garnished with the coriander and mint.

Onion and Red Pepper Kachumber

Kachumbers are the quickest and easiest of salads. This one is crunchy and fresh.

1 ONION, FINELY CHOPPED
½ RED PEPPER
½ YELLOW PEPPER
1 TABLESPOON CHOPPED FRESH CORIANDER
1 TEASPOON SESAME SEEDS
½ TABLESPOON LEMON JUICE

Deseed the peppers and chop them finely. Place in a serving bowl and mix in the onion and coriander. Sprinkle with sesame seeds and the lemon juice. Serve immediately.

VARIATION
Kachumber with Chickpeas, Tomato, Onion and Peppers
Add 1 large, sliced tomato and a few tablespoons of canned chickpeas, if liked, to the recipe above. Serve immediately.

Guava Kachumber

Guavas are becoming more widely available in the larger supermarkets, and you will certainly find them in Asian and oriental greengrocers. Their scent, when ripe, is utterly wonderful – it's worth buying them and just keeping them in a fruit bowl to enjoy their fragrance. Better than roses! They are usually eaten fresh, but they make a delicious kachumber. This one can be eaten by itself, like a chaat.

6 GUAVAS
1 TEASPOON RED CHILLI POWDER
2 TABLESPOONS LEMON JUICE
½ TEASPOON SALT
2 TEASPOONS SUGAR
FRESHLY GROUND BLACK PEPPER
1 TABLESPOON CHOPPED FRESH MINT, TO GARNISH

Do not peel the guavas, or you will lose their lovely scent. Chop into large dice, or slice like tomatoes. Sprinkle over the chilli powder, lemon juice, salt and sugar, and mix gently. Sprinkle with freshly ground black pepper and the chopped fresh mint, to garnish.

VARIATION
Banana Kachumber
Substitute 2–3 ripe bananas, sliced, for the guavas, and then proceed as in the main recipe.

Bundi in Masala Yogurt

Bundi, which is made from lentil flour, is widely available from Indian and Pakistani supermarkets.It is used to make this yogurt-based accompaniment,which is delicious and versatile.

250 ML (8 FL OZ) NATURAL YOGURT
1 TEASPOON SALT
1 TABLESPOON SUGAR
50 ML (2 FL OZ) WATER
½ TEASPOON GROUND CORIANDER
½ TEASPOON CHILLI POWER
1 TABLESPOON CHOPPED FRESH CORIANDER
1 TABLESPOON OIL
¼ TEASPOON ONION SEEDS
¼ TEASPOON WHITE CUMIN SEEDS
3 DRIED RED CHILLIES
50 G (2 OZ) BUNDI

Whisk the yogurt and add the salt, sugar, water, ground coriander, chilli powder and chopped coriander and set aside.

Heat the oil in a small frying pan and fry the onion seeds, white cumin seeds and dried red chillies. Remove from the heat and set aside for a few seconds while you pour the bundi into the yogurt and mix it in well.

Pour the oil dressing over the yogurt mixture and serve.
NOTE: You may immerse the bundi in hot water for a few seconds to soften it before adding it to the yogurt.

Spicy Dip

Another dip to use with starters, or with poppadums or nibbles at a drinks party.

250 G (8 OZ) GREEK YOGURT
1GREEN CHILLI, CHOPPED
1 TEASPOON SALT
1 TABLESPOON FRESH CORIANDER
½ CUCUMBER, ROUGHLY CHOPPED
125 ML (4 FL OZ) SINGLE CREAM
1 TEASPOON FRESH MINT LEAVES
TO GARNISH
SPRIG OF MINT
SPRIG OF CORIANDER

Place the Greek yogurt, chilli, salt, fresh coriander, cucumber, single cream and fresh mint in a food processor and whisk for about 40 seconds.

Transfer to a serving bowl and serve garnished with the mint and coriander.

Hot Mango Pickle

Unripe or green mangoes should be used for pickles. They usually arrive in the shops in this state, so choose the greenest you can find. Pickles are usually quite hot, and so should be eaten in very small quantities.

5 LARGE UNRIPE MANGOES, UNPEELED
2 TABLESPOONS SALT
3–4 TABLESPOONS CORN OIL
½ TEASPOON ONION SEEDS
½ TEASPOON MUSTARD SEEDS
¼ TEASPOON FENUGREEK SEEDS
¼ TEASPOON CRUSHED CORIANDER SEEDS
¼ TEASPOON WHITE CUMIN SEEDS
¼ TEASPOON FENNEL SEEDS
¼ TEASPOON CRUSHED DRIED RED CHILLIES
2.5 CM (1 INCH) FRESH ROOT GINGER, GRATED
2 CURRY LEAVES
1 TEASPOON CHILLI POWDER
¼ TEASPOON TURMERIC
1½ TEASPOONS GROUND CORIANDER
1 TEASPOON SALT

Wash the mangoes and cut into 2.5 cm (1 inch) pieces, discarding the seeds. Rub the salt on the pieces and leave overnight. Squeeze out all the liquid from the pieces, then leave to dry for a minimum of 6 hours.

Heat the oil and fry all the whole spices for about 1 minute. Remove from the heat and add the chilli powder, turmeric, ground coriander and salt. Blend everything together, then add the mango pieces. Return to the heat and stir-fry for about 2 minutes.

Set aside to cool, then store in airtight containers.

Spicy Tomato Ketchup

This dip can be served as a starter with vegetable crudités, or as an accompaniment to other dishes.

6 TABLESPOONS TOMATO KETCHUP
1 TEASPOON LEMON JUICE
½ TEASPOON CHILLI POWDER
SALT
1 TEASPOON FINELY CHOPPED FRESH CORIANDER

Mix all the ingredients together and serve.

Aubergine Bhurta

Beautiful, glossy purple aubergines are native to India, and were taken to Europe as early as the 14th Century. There is also a white form, which gave rise to their alternative name, 'eggplant'. They range in size from the heavy, large ones used in this recipe, to long thin curved ones – which look pretty when used in vegetable dishes – to little round white ones, just like large hens' eggs. Bhurta is eaten as an accompaniment all over India, but perhaps more in the north. Though it can be made with other vegetables, aubergines are probably the most popular.

1 LARGE AUBERGINE
SALT
1 TEASPOON SALT
3 GREEN CHILLIES, FINELY CHOPPED
1 ONION, FINELY CHOPPED
2 TOMATOES, FINELY CHOPPED
2 TABLESPOONS OIL
½ TEASPOON ONION SEEDS
4 CURRY LEAVES
175 G (6 OZ) NATURAL YOGURT
2 TABLESPOONS CHOPPED FRESH CORIANDER
2 TABLESPOONS CHOPPED FRESH MINT

Peel the aubergine, chop roughly and cook in lightly salted boiling water until soft and mushy. Drain the aubergine well and place in a serving dish.

Mix the chillies, onion and tomatoes into the aubergine.

Heat the oil in a small pan, add the onion seeds and curry leaves and fry for 2–3 minutes, or until they turn a shade darker. Pour the hot, spiced oil over the aubergine.

Whisk the yogurt and add the coriander and mint. Pour the mixture over the bhurta.

VARIATION
Cucumber Bhurta, Doodhi or Marrow Bhurta
Other vegetables may be used instead of the aubergine. Replace the aubergine with a doodhi or marrow, or 2 large cucumbers, and proceed as in the main recipe.

Desserts

Desserts and sweetmeats are most often served as special dishes for festive occasions like weddings and other family celebrations. While this chapter includes two recipes for halva, the sweetmeat for religious festivals, there are also more every-day sweet rice dishes, and a recipe for lassi, the cooling yogurt-based drink.

Chana Dhaal Halva

This is a traditional recipe, made quite regularly in some Muslim households. It is also stuffed in puris and the puris are then fried and served with kheer (rice pudding). However, served on its own as a dessert it is delicious.

250 G (8 OZ) CHANA DHAAL
900 ML (1½ PINTS) WATER
5 TABLESPOONS PURE GHEE
3 GREEN CARDAMOMS, CRUSHED
4 WHOLE CLOVES
175 G (6 OZ) GROUND ALMONDS
300–375 G (10–12 OZ) SUGAR
1 TEASPOON SAFFRON STRANDS
75 G (3 OZ) SULTANAS
SLIVERED ALMONDS, TO GARNISH

Wash the dhaal and pick over for any stones etc. Place in a medium heavy-based saucepan with the water. Bring to the boil, lower the heat and cook until the dhaal is soft enough to be mashed.

Drain well and discard the water, then transfer the dhaal to a liquidizer or food processor and blend to form a paste-like consistency. If necessary, add up to 150 ml (¼ pint) water to form the required consistency.

Heat the ghee in a large saucepan, then add the crushed cardamom seeds and cloves. Lower the heat and add the chana dhaal paste and start stirring and mixing together gently, using the *bhoono-ing* method (see page 9).

Continue to stir-fry, scraping the bottom of the pan, for about 5–7 minutes. Gradually fold the ground almonds into the mixture and continue to stir-fry for a further 5–7 minutes.

Next fold in the sugar, saffron and sultanas and mix well.

The halva should now have become darker. Continue to stir-fry for another 2 minutes. Remove the pan from the heat and transfer to a serving dish.

Decorate the halva with slivered almonds. It may be served hot or cold, with cream if preferred.

Almond and Semolina Halva
(Badam Aur Sooji Ka Halva)

300–375 G (10–12 OZ) SUGAR
1 LITRE (1¾ PINTS) WATER
3 TABLESPOONS PURE GHEE
3 GREEN CARDAMOMS
2 CLOVES
150 G (5 OZ) COARSE SEMOLINA
175 G (6 OZ) GROUND ALMONDS
½ TEASPOON SAFFRON STRANDS
50 G (2 OZ) SULTANAS
TO GARNISH
1 TABLESPOON SLIVERED ALMONDS
1 TABLESPOON PISTACHIO NUTS
2 SHEETS VARQ

Place the sugar and 450 ml (¾ pint) of the water in a large saucepan and bring to the boil. Continue to boil until you have a thick syrup.

Meanwhile, melt the ghee in a heavy-based saucepan. Add the cardamoms and cloves and stir-fry for about 10 seconds.

Mix the semolina and almonds together and add them to the hot ghee. Lower the heat to medium. Stir-fry for about 5 minutes. Add the saffron strands and sultanas and stir-fry or a further 2 minutes.

Pour in the remaining water and cook over a low heat, stirring occasionally.

Once the syrup is ready, pour it into the halva and cook until the syrup is fully absorbed and the halva is a golden colour.

Transfer the halva to a serving dish and serve garnished with the almonds, pistachio nuts and varq. Serve the halva with cream, too, if liked.

Lassi

This delightfully cool drink makes a refreshing accompaniment to hot and spicy curries. Lassis are, traditionally, either salt or sweet. This one is sweet, and the saffron flavouring is unusual but delicious.

300 G (10 OZ) NATURAL YOGURT
600 ML (1 PINT) WATER
4–6 TABLESPOONS SUGAR
LARGE PINCH OF POWDERED SAFFRON,
PLUS EXTRA TO DECORATE

Put the yogurt in a jug and whisk with a wire whisk for about 2 minutes. Pour in the water, sugar and saffron and continue to whisk for a further 3–5 minutes. Serve chilled, with an extra pinch of saffron sprinkled over the top.

PREVIOUS PAGES: *From left, Saffron Kheer (Zafrani Kheer), (recipe page 121), and Almond and Semolina Halva (Bedam aur Sooji Ka Halva), decorated with almonds and pistachios (recipe above, right). Indians have an incorrigibly sweet tooth, especially for sweetmeats. These desserts are just a selection of the many marvellous puddings to be found in the various regional Indian cuisines.*

Ground Rice Pudding
(Firni)

50 G (2 OZ) GROUND RICE

50 G (2 OZ) GROUND ALMONDS

900 ML (1½ PINTS) MILK

2 CARDAMOM SEEDS, CRUSHED

6–8 TABLESPOONS SUGAR

1 TEASPOON KEWRA WATER (OPTIONAL)

TO GARNISH

4–6 PISTACHIO NUTS, SLICED

4–6 ALMONDS, SLIVERED

2 VARQ LEAVES (OPTIONAL)

Mix the ground rice and ground almonds together. Pour into a saucepan and gradually add 600 ml (1 pint) of the milk, whisking continually to prevent any balls forming.

Add the cardamom seeds and cook over a low heat for at least 15 minutes, stirring occasionally.

Add the sugar and the remaining milk. Continue to cook, stirring occasionally to prevent the mixture from catching on the bottom of the pan, until it has thickened.

Once the pudding has thickened to about the consistency of a thick soup, stir in the kewra water, if using, and transfer the pudding to a serving dish. Garnish with the pistachio nuts, almonds and varq, if using.

The pudding may be served hot or cold.

Gujarati-style Rice Pudding

50 G (2 OZ) BASMATI RICE

1.2 LITRES (2 PINTS) MILK

50 G (2 OZ) GROUND ALMONDS

4 GREEN CARDAMOMS

4 TABLESPOONS SUGAR

25 G (1 OZ) SLIVERED ALMONDS, TO DECORATE

Wash the rice thoroughly. Drain and set aside. Pour the milk into a large saucepan and bring to the boil. Add the rice and cook over a medium heat for about 10 minutes. Add the ground almonds and cardamoms and cook until the milk is reduced to half its quantity.

Add the sugar and continue cooking, stirring, for a further 5 minutes.

Transfer the pudding to a serving dish, decorate with slivered almonds and serve. The cardamoms may be removed before serving, but this is not necessary.

Saffron Kheer
(Zafrani Kheer)

½ CUP BASMATI RICE

2 TABLESPOONS PURE GHEE

3 GREEN CARDAMOMS

1 TABLESPOON GROUND ALMONDS

1 TEASPOON SAFFRON STRANDS

1.5 LITRES (2½ PINTS) FULL CREAM MILK

8–10 TABLESPOONS SUGAR

TO GARNISH

25 G (1 OZ) FLAKED ALMONDS

1 OR 2 VARQ LEAVES (OPTIONAL)

Coarsely grind the rice in a food processor and set aside.

Heat the ghee in a large saucepan and fry the cardamoms for a few seconds. Lower the heat, add the ground almonds, rice and saffron strands and stir-fry for about 1 minute.

Remove the pan from the heat and pour in the milk, stirring continuously to prevent any balls forming. Return to the heat and bring to the boil. Lower the heat and cook until reduced by half. Add the sugar and cook for 5–7 minutes more, stirring occasionally to prevent it from sticking to the pan.

Remove from the heat, transfer a serving dish and garnish with the almonds and varq, if using.

Coconut and Rice Payasham

125 G (4 OZ) BASMATI RICE

1.5 LITRES (2½ PINTS) MILK

½ TEASPOON CRUSHED CARDAMOM SEEDS

125 G (4 OZ) DESICCATED COCONUT

250–300 G (8–10 OZ) SUGAR

2 TABLESPOONS ROSEWATER

8–10 PISTACHIO NUTS, CHOPPED

10–12 FLAKED ALMOND PIECES

Wash the rice, drain well and place in a saucepan with 900 ml (1½ pints) of the milk, the cardamoms and coconut.

Place the pan, partly covered, over a medium heat and cook for 35–40 minutes, or until the rice is soft enough to be mashed and most of the milk has been absorbed. Remove from the heat, mash the rice, add the sugar and the remaining milk.

Return to the heat and bring to the boil, stirring occasionally. Continue cooking for 5–7 minutes then pour in the rosewater.

Transfer to a heatproof dish. Decorate with the pistachio nuts and flaked almonds. Serve chilled.

Equipment

You probably already have in your kitchen almost all the equipment you will need for cooking Indian food. Good-quality, heavy-based saucepans and a frying pan, some wooden spatulas and a slotted spoon for stirring rice, are the first essentials. If you have a Chinese wok, that can also be a good substitute for the karahi or balti pan.

You should also have good, sharp knives, kitchen scales, measuring spoons and a measuring jug.

In an Indian kitchen you would probably also find a rice cooker and perhaps a garlic press, as well as more traditional equipment. Suggestions are:

Thawa
A slightly concave griddle or frying pan, usually made of cast-iron, is used for cooking chapatis and paratas and for roasting spices. An ordinary frying pan makes the perfect substitute – use a small one, about 12 cm (5 inches) for dry-roasting spices (see page 8).

Karahi
Sometimes spelt *karihai* or *kadhai*. This is a deep frying pan which resembles a straight-sided wok, with handles on both sides. It is made from various metals and alloys, the most common of which are iron, aluminium and stainless steel. You can substitute a Chinese wok or a good-quality, large frying pan.

Balti pans
Balti cooking is becoming increasingly popular, and balti pans are now widely available. They are almost identical to the karahi, though their name means 'bucket'. If you don't have an authentic balti pan, a wok, karahi or deep frying pan makes a perfectly acceptable substitute.

Girda
A small pastry board, 25 cm (10 inch) in diameter, with short legs, used for rolling out dough. You can substitute an ordinary wooden cutting board, or your normal surface for working pastry.

Food Processor or Liquidizer
Traditionally, Indian households would use a grinding stone for preparing spices and grinding flours. In modern kitchens, these tasks have been taken over by the food processor and liquidizer.

Spice Grinder
A traditional Indian cook would grind her spices on the grinding stone. You could substitute a mortar and pestle or a rolling pin, but the best modern substitute in both Asian and European kitchens is a coffee grinder, kept just for grinding spices (otherwise coffee ground in it would acquire a rather peppery, spicy taste). A food processor is just too large to cope with the small quantities of spices needed for home-cooked curries.

Spice box
An Indian cook keeps spices in a Spice Box beside the stove. She uses spices every day and so uses them quickly, before they have time to go stale. You should buy small quantities and keep them in airtight bottles in a cool, dark place. You could also keep them, tightly sealed, in the refrigerator if you have space.

Rolling pin
For rolling out chapati and other doughs. In many Indian households, the flat, heavy grindstone and a *mussal*, which is rather like a rolling pin, are used.

Garlic press
Use a garlic press if you have one. Alternatively, crush the cloves with the flat of a large knife and remove the papery covering. Drop a few grains of salt over the smashed clove and mash carefully with the flat, pointed end of the knife. The clove will be puréed in a matter of seconds, with no waste. For puréeing larger amounts of garlic see page 9.

Rice cookers
Electric rice cookers have become popular throughout the East, wherever rice is cooked regularly and in large quantities, because they ensure that the rice is always perfectly cooked and will stay warm until required, without burning. They aren't absolutely essential, but if you cook rice often I think it's worth buying one.

RIGHT: *From the top, Panir and Vegetable Roghan Josh (recipe page 70), and Stir-fry Cabbage with Green Mango (recipe page 71). Unusual vegetable combinations give extra interest to these curries.*

Index

Page numbers in *italic* refer to the illustrations